MANPOWER SERVICES COMMISSION

Classification of Occupations and Directory of Occupational Titles

VOLUME 1
Introduction/Structure/Index

LONDON: HER MAJESTY'S STATIONERY OFFICE

_ Ha 78547/2

ACKNOWLEDGEMENTS

The Department of Employment gratefully
acknowledges the considerable assistance which
many employers, workers and their
associations and other organisations and
individuals have given with the preparation
of this classification, by allowing job studies
to be carried out in their establishments, by
supplying information, by commenting on
drafts and by making constructive suggestions.
Without such assistance the preparation of
this publication would not have been possible.
The Department, nevertheless, accepts full
responsibility for the classification.

HER MAJESTY'S STATIONERY OFFICE

Government Bookshops

49 High Holborn, London WC1V 6HB
13a Castle Street, Edinburgh EH2 3AR
41 The Hayes, Cardiff CF1 1JW
Brazennose Street, Manchester M60 8AS
Southey House, Wine Street, Bristol BS1 2BQ
258 Broad Street, Birmingham B1 2HE
80 Chichester Street, Belfast BT1 4JY
*Government publications are also available
through booksellers*

ISBN 0 11 885306 6*

CONTENTS

COI-A*

PREFACE

Occupational classification is such an important aid to manpower utilisation and planning that the Department of Employment, with the help of many organisations and individuals, has developed and compiled this new CLASSIFICATION OF OCCUPATIONS AND DIRECTORY OF OCCUPATIONAL TITLES (CODOT). It will be used in the Department's employment and career guidance services and it is hoped that it will also prove valuable to others who wish to identify and classify occupations. Codification of all the occupations in which workers have had experience, together with a suitable retrieval system, can help employers to achieve the best deployment of labour within their organisations. No single occupational classification system can completely satisfy the requirements of every potential user, but to make CODOT useful over as wide an area as possible the classification has been made simple to operate and broadly compatible with other national and international classifications.

CODOT will also serve as an information system in the collection and analysis of statistics. The Department has studied the occupations for which statistics are required by the Government and by Industrial Training Boards and in an attempt to standardise, has drawn up a "list of key occupations for statistical purposes" (see page 89). All key list occupations are defined in CODOT and are grouped in the same broad structure. Generally, occupations included in future statistical enquiries will also be identified by their CODOT occupational number, thus simplifying the completion of Government returns for those employers who use the classification.

The base material for the occupational definitions was obtained from some 20,000 job studies involving observations of and interviews with workers, from information supplied by organisations and from various other sources.

Occupations are generally defined in broad terms. Variations in the tasks performed occur between one place of employment and another and consequently not all definitions can be expected to coincide exactly with specific jobs in a particular establishment or in a given locality.

When collecting data about occupations no information was obtained about hours worked, pay received or similar matters. The definitions of occupations should not be regarded as authoritative descriptions of the duties of a particular worker and the classification should not be regarded as setting any standard or relative level in respect of pay, hours of work or related subjects.

AMENDMENT OF CODOT

Changes occur in industrial practice as a result of scientific discoveries, use of new materials, improved methods of production, manpower utilisation agreements etc. In consequence, new occupations will arise for which separate classifications have not been provided or the range of duties undertaken by workers in an existing occupation may be enlarged or curtailed. The Careers and Occupational Information Centre (Manpower Services Commission), 3 St Andrew's Place, Regents Park, London NW1 4LB, would welcome information on such changes, which will be taken into account in the periodical up-dating of CODOT. Supplements giving amplifications and amendments will be published and will incorporate entries in earlier supplements, so that at any one time there will be only one supplement current.

Some occupational titles, phrases or individual words in this publication may refer to a worker or workers of a particular sex but they should not be taken to imply that the occupation/career is restricted to one sex unless the occupation is excluded from the general provisions of the Sex Discrimination Act.

INTRODUCTION

BASIS AND STRUCTURE OF THE CLASSIFICATION

Basis

CODOT provides a classification system to cover all occupations found in Great Britain but distinctions between occupations are generally made only when they are considered to be of value for employment or statistical purposes. This results in about 3,500 separately identified occupations plus a number of residual occupations.

The following definitions are adopted:

> JOB   all the tasks carried out by a particular worker to complete his duties.

> OCCUPATION   a collection of jobs sufficiently similar in their main tasks to be grouped under a common title for classification purposes.

In general this means that workers in a particular CODOT occupation should be able to undertake all the jobs covered by that occupation with little or no further training.

Occupations are identified and grouped primarily in terms of the work usually performed, this being determined by the tasks, duties and responsibilities of the occupation. Factors such as the materials processed or worked, the machinery and tools used, the products made and services provided, substitution and promotion, have all been taken as indications of the work performed, when combining jobs into occupations and occupations into larger groups.

Occupations are not therefore identified and grouped primarily in terms of the industry in which the worker is employed nor by his level of authority, skill or qualifications, because these are regarded as additional facets of occupations. However, these facets are implicit in some CODOT occupational groupings, for example:

(a) occupations which are specific to an individual industry are grouped together

(b) levels of authority between worker and supervisor, between supervisor and manager and between manager and general manager are recognised because they are reflected in the nature of the work performed

(c) grouping by work performed inevitably brings together many occupations of similar skill levels

(d) qualifications are usually mentioned when they have some legal significance (eg in medicine, law, aircraft piloting), but in general the performance of tasks and duties takes precedence over possession of formal qualifications.

The principle of identifying and grouping occupations according to work performed is followed in two other standard works, the International Standard Classification of Occupations (ISCO) and the classification used by the Office of Population Censuses and Surveys for analysis of census data. The three classifications therefore have considerable compatibility.

Structure

The 3,500 occupations are grouped at three levels to show wider occupational relationships and to identify groups of general significance for manpower planning. These levels are:

UNIT GROUP   a basic group of occupations in which the main tasks are similar or have many similar characteristics. Generally speaking therefore, a unit group has an occupational homogeneity and the occupations in it are more closely related to each other in terms of work performed than to occupations outside the group.

MINOR GROUP   a collection of unit groups which are related in terms of work performed and/or reflect a corporate activity commonly found in the employment field.

MAJOR GROUP   a convenient collection of minor groups to assist in comprehension of the classification as a whole.

There are 378 unit groups, 73 minor groups and 18 major groups. The 3,500 occupations are therefore structured in a four tier system of classification which can be operated at different levels of refinement to suit the varying needs of users. Gaps are left throughout the code numbering system so that finer distinctions between occupations or groups can be introduced to suit particular needs of users without impairing the coding system as a whole.

CODOT STRUCTURE IN RELATION TO COMPANY ORGANISATION

The broad structure of the classification is based on the organisational pattern of many large manufacturing companies, with top or general management at the beginning, followed by professional and related specialist occupations supporting top management and frequently found in headquarters offices, and then by technical, scientific and other specialist occupations engaged in background work. These are followed by line management and the production and service occupations under their control. The relationship of CODOT's structure to company organisation is indicated in the chart [on pages 10 and 11], which shows a synthesised model of the organisation of a large manufacturing company together with appropriate CODOT code numbers.

TITLES, DEFINITIONS AND CODE NUMBERS

General

For reference, the group structure of the classification is given on page 21, followed by a classified list of titles and code numbers of major, minor and unit groups and of occupations. Volumes II and III contain the definitions of groups and of occupations.

Titles

To emphasise that CODOT is a classification of occupations rather than of workers, the titles of major and minor groups include the word 'occupations'. However, worker titles are given to all individual occupations and also to those unit groups for which such titles are in common use, for example pharmacists, draughtsmen, tailors.

Titles of occupations are intended to reflect activities or work performed rather than qualifications so that titles such as accountant and joiner are used in preference to chartered accountant and craftsman. As far as it is consistent with this general principle, the titles chosen are those in common use. With a few exceptions, occupations are given only one main title but other titles are included at the end of the relevant definitions and occasionally in the 'may' items (see page 9). To avoid repetition, qualifying terms used in the main title are omitted from the other titles, but they are regarded as implicit.

Occasionally an occupation covers two or more quite separate but closely linked jobs. In these cases the occupation is given a generic title and the separate job definitions are indented under the main title.

Because such terms as head, chief, senior have a variety of meanings, they are used in CODOT titles only when they reflect a distinction in the work performed. Trade names are also avoided wherever possible.

A number of occupations are commonly known by titles which include the term 'assistant'. In general these occupations are separately identified only when the function of the assistant is distinct from that of the worker he is assisting. Most of these cases occur when the title ends with the term assistant; for example a textile printer's assistant is separately identified but an assistant manager is classified as a manager.

Definitions

Following the title of each major and minor group there is a brief general definition of the type of work included in the group and a list of the code numbers and titles of its component minor and unit groups respectively. Following each unit group title is a more detailed description of the work covered by the occupations in the group.

Occupational definitions come after unit group definitions and include five basic components:

(1) FLAG STATEMENT – a short opening statement giving the essential characteristics of the occupation in terms of the work performed.

(2) HOW ITEMS – a series of short statements describing the main tasks normally carried out in the occupation. On occasions, these are replaced by a cross reference to a base definition or to the definition of a closely related occupation, thereby avoiding repetition of the main tasks common to a number of occupations.

(3) MAY ITEMS – when appropriate, a few short statements, indicating common specialisations within the occupation and tasks additional to those implicit in the flag statement which are often associated with the occupation.

(4) as necessary, a statement of ADDITIONAL FACTORS which are of importance when considering employment in the occupation.

(5) OTHER TITLES which are used for various jobs covered by the occupation. Although not exhaustive, these cover the majority of titles in use for the particular occupation.

An example of the content of an occupational definition is given below:

Occupational number and title ⋯⋯▶	**311.15 Cost clerk**
Flag statement ⋯⋯⋯⋯⋯⋯⋯⋯▶	Calculates estimated or final costs, or one or more factors of the cost of a product or service.
How item ⋯⋯⋯⋯⋯⋯⋯⋯⋯⋯▶	Examines records such as time and production sheets, payrolls, operations charts and schedules, and extracts data for calculations; calculates actual or estimated cost of individual items such as labour, materials and time costs, overhead expenses; prepares analyses, statements, or comparisons of unit or total costs as required.
May item ⋯⋯⋯⋯⋯⋯⋯⋯⋯⋯▶	May (01) specialise in the calculation of production costs for budgetary control purposes and be known as Budgetary control clerk.
Additional factor ⋯⋯⋯⋯⋯⋯▶	Knowledge of a particular costing method such as contract, prime, standard or unit costing.
Other titles ⋯⋯⋯⋯⋯⋯⋯⋯▶	Cost and works accountant's clerk, Cost control clerk, Estimating clerk, Production and cost control clerk.

Group and occupational definitions are also followed, where appropriate, by notes, cross references, inclusions and exclusions.

CODOT in relation to Company organisation (manufacturing)

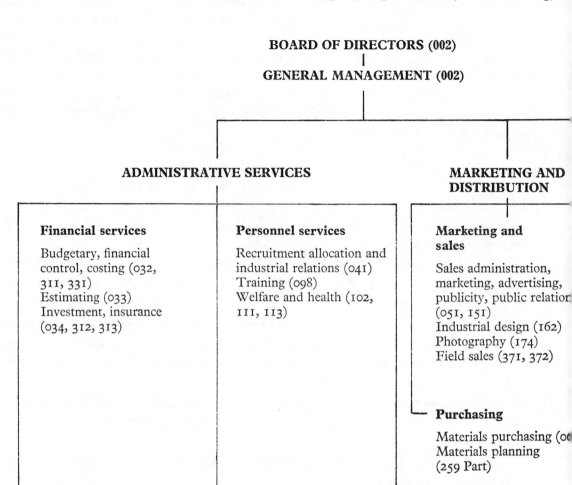

BOARD OF DIRECTORS (002)

GENERAL MANAGEMENT (002)

ADMINISTRATIVE SERVICES

Financial services

Budgetary, financial control, costing (032, 311, 331)
Estimating (033)
Investment, insurance (034, 312, 313)

Personnel services

Recruitment allocation and industrial relations (041)
Training (098)
Welfare and health (102, 111, 113)

MARKETING AND DISTRIBUTION

Marketing and sales

Sales administration, marketing, advertising, publicity, public relations (051, 151)
Industrial design (162)
Photography (174)
Field sales (371, 372)

Purchasing

Materials purchasing (0
Materials planning (259 Part)

General administrative services

Legal (022)
Company secretarial (031)
Property management (062)
Records, library, information (063, 316)

Management services

Operational research, O & M, work study (042)
Economics, statistics (043)
Computer services (044, 332, 333)

Common services†

*Office management (281, 289 (part))
*General clerical services (319 (part), 32, 334)
Communications (281, 34)
Catering (284, 43)
Security (288, 41)
Cleaning (289 (part), 452)

NOTES

1 This chart is a synthesised model developed after examination of the structure of a number of large manufacturing firms. It may not have a parallel in any actual company but should be adaptable to the structure of most companies, even those outside manufacturing, to which it would not apply in full.

2 CODOT minor or unit group reference numbers are shown in brackets. For the sake of brevity, all supervisory and most residual groups have been omitted.

3 As CODOT groups occupations in terms of work performed, not all the occupations involving the same tasks are located in the same section of the company organisation.

PRODUCTION

Materials control and movement

Warehousing, storekeeping (277, 314, 951)
Packaging (277, 84)
Materials handling and moving (internal) (277, 942, 959 (part))
Transporting, despatch (277, 315, 92, 93)

Production management

Works management production control (271, 272, 276)

Production operations

Materials processing (53-59, 71)
Manufacturing (61-69, 72, 73, 75, 77, 79, 812-815)
Assembly (repetitive) (82)
Inspection (83)
Utility services (971, 972)

Research and development

Technical and scientific research, development, design etc (211, 212, 213, 215, 223, 224, 225, 231, 254, 256)
Production engineering and planning, technical quality control, technical service advice (226, 259 (part))
Drawing office (253)

Installation, maintenance and repair

Machinery and plant installation, maintenance and repair (256, 273, 74, 76)
Building maintenance (274, 671, 673, 771, 811, 86)
Maintenance of grounds and gardens (504)

*OFFICE MANAGEMENT AND CLERICAL SERVICES

Office management and general clerical services (including typing, secretarial and some machine operating services) are common to many of the functional areas above, eg legal, sales etc. To avoid needless repetition, they have been included under Common Services. Clerical and machine operating services specific to particular functional areas have been included in those areas, eg costing and accounting clerical occupations (311) are shown under Financial Services.

†COMMON SERVICES

There is no generally accepted position in a company organisation for certain functions such as security and catering and these have therefore been grouped together under Common Services.

INTRODUCTION

Unit groups contain a residual occupation, worded in general terms, to provide for occupations which fall within the group definition but are not separately identified. Commonly used titles appropriate to residual occupations are listed as examples, together with a defining phrase when the title is not self-explanatory. Major and minor groups contain residual minor and unit groups whenever appropriate.

Code Numbers

A decimal system of code numbering is used. Minor groups are given code numbers of two digits within the range 00 to 99 and unit groups a code number of three digits within the range 001 to 999, the first two digits being those of the minor group to which the unit group belongs. Occupations are given two digits additional to the unit group number and separated from it by a point (.), so that occupational numbers consist of five digits. The following example illustrates this code numbering:

Minor group **31**　　　Clerical occupations

Unit group　**310**　　Supervisors (clerical occupations)

Occupation　**310 .10**　Supervisor (costing and accounting clerical occupations)

Each minor group has provision for up to 10 unit groups and each unit group can accommodate up to 100 occupations.

Major groups cannot be represented by single digits because CODOT has more than ten major groups. Accordingly roman numerals I to XVIII are used, but major groups can also be identified by using the two digit arabic numerals of their first and last constituent minor groups (for example 61–69 for major group XIII).

Supervisory occupations are identified at unit group level within the code numbering system. All unit groups ending third digit 0 relate exclusively to supervisors and foremen.

Fourth and fifth digits in the range .00 to .97 are used for specific occupations. The digits are allocated at intervals depending on the number of definitions to be accommodated. Trainees are given occupational numbers ending .98 within the unit group containing the occupations for which they are being trained. Trainee accountants are therefore classified 032 .98. Residual occupations have an occupational number ending .99, for example 722 .99 other machine tool setter-operators.

Special treatment is given to certain scientific, technical and managerial occupations, so that all workers who have the same function or work with the same product or material can be readily identified. Each fourth digit is used to represent a specific functional characteristic (eg research and development) and each fifth digit to represent the field with which the worker is involved (eg heavy chemicals). This applies to the unit groups for chemical scientists (212), civil and structural, mechanical, electrical and electronic, and chemical engineers (221, 223, 224 and 225), certain engineering supporting occupations (256) and certain operational managers (271 and 272). A summary of the contents of these groups is given immediately following the unit group definition and a specimen is reproduced on page 13. For consistency of presentation each possible combination of fourth and fifth digit specialisations is separately coded and defined.

For many purposes it will be adequate to use two, three or five digit code numbers, but each of the may items is given a two digit number so that the specialisation or additional tasks recorded in them can be identified by code number if necessary. Thus for example an analytical chemist (chemical and related products) (212 .51) has the additional digits (08) if he specialises in explosives. For the same reason occupations indented under a main occupation and specific titles of residual occupations are also given two additional digits. Two digits are used rather than one because some occupations are given more than 10 specialisations and users may wish to codify the information for use on a computer.

Mechanical Engineer 223		General mech-anical engin-eering	Prime movers	Mech-anical instru-ments	Aircraft and missile structures	Vehicle chassis and bodies	Ships' structures	Mech-anical plant, machinery and equip-ment	Other mech-anical engin-eering
		.–1	.–2	.–3	.–4	.–5	.–6	.–7	.–9
General	.1–								
Research and development	.2–								
Design	.3–								
Feasibility studies	.4–								
Applications	.5–								
Liaison	.6–								
Consultancy and advice	.7–								

.00 Manager
.98 Trainee
.99 Other mechanical engineering research and development, design, feasibility studies, applications, liaison, consultancy and related occupations.

Examples: Mechanical engineer (research and development) (mechanical instruments)   223.23
Mechanical engineer (applications) (prime movers)   223.52

NOTES ON CLASSIFYING OCCUPATIONS

Occupational titles are not a satisfactory guide to occupational classification because the same occupational title may be used to describe workers performing widely different tasks and conversely different occupational titles may be used for the same type of work. Occupational classification should therefore be determined according to the work performed. The following examples illustrate this:

a) Some shop assistants who sell meat might describe themselves as butchers but butchers who prepare meat are classified in CODOT separately from shop assistants who are engaged in selling meat.

(b) The title information officer is frequently applied to a number of occupations or jobs such as public relations officer, press officer, book editor and publicity writer. These occupations are separately identified in CODOT.

(c) CODOT differentiates between product inspectors and testers who use judgment based on lengthy experience or training and product examiners, viewers and checkers who require little or no training. These titles are often used interchangeably by firms.

(d) In many production areas CODOT separately identifies four types of machine workers ie setters, setter-operators, operators and attendants/minders. Equally distinctions are often drawn between occupations involving working by hand or with machine.

These distinctions have validity in terms of work performed but they are often not obvious from the occupational titles normally used. It is therefore important in classifying an occupation to ensure that the flag statement of the occupation thought appropriate satisfactorily describes the work performed. If it does not, a further search of the index should be made. If this proves abortive, the structure shown on pages 21 to 31 should be examined until the appropriate group and occupation is identified.

Provided the flag statement satisfactorily defines the work performed, classification to a particular occupation is valid even if a few of the how items are not appropriate.

Even though occupations are defined in broad terms, individual jobs may straddle two or more CODOT occupations. This problem is aggravated by the growing trend towards occupational flexibility, typified by workers trained to do two or more previously distinct occupations. CODOT helps reduce the number of straddlers by:

(a) referring in may items to other occupations whose duties may be performed in full or in part; for example plumber (771 .05) is given a may item to identify the plumber who does glazing

(b) providing a general occupation for those who perform a variety of tasks, for example an engineering fitter-assembler (general) (733 .05) who can perform more than one of the specialist fitter-assembler occupations (machine tools, aircraft engines etc)

(c) identifying multi-skilled occupations which combine functions from more than one unit group and which appear sufficiently important to justify separate classification, for example mechanical *and* electrical maintenance fitters (799 .04); setter-operators of woodcutting *and* metal working machines (799 .06).

Despite these provisions, there will still be jobs which straddle CODOT occupations. These should be classified to the occupation covering the major component of the work performed, or where this is not appropriate, to the most relevant residual group.

When using CODOT to record worker experience for employment placement, or for other purposes where identification of specific skills is necessary, it may be advantageous to allot more than one occupation number to a worker whose experience straddles two or three occupations and to reserve the general occupation for those workers whose experience might truly be so described.

NOTES ON CLASSIFICATION OF MANAGERS, WORKING PRINCIPALS, SUPERVISORS/FOREMEN, NATIONAL AND LOCAL GOVERNMENT OFFICIALS, MEMBERS OF THE ARMED FORCES, TRAINEES AND LABOURERS

Managers

The title manager is often loosely applied to a variety of occupations, some of which might be regarded as managerial in one organisation and as supervisory or specialist in another. Frequently managerial occupations involve duties quite dissimilar in nature, for example, managers of small retail shops and general managers of large industrial concerns. Moreover managerial occupations are sometimes known by a variety of other titles such as director, chief or superintendant.

In CODOT the manager is regarded as one whose prime function is to plan, organise, co-ordinate and control work and resources, usually through other managers or through supervisors, whilst supervisors are regarded as those who are in immediate day-to-day control of basic production and service workers. Those entitled general foremen who have other foremen under their control are classified in managerial groups but on the other hand, some occupations which have the title of manager do not entail managerial functions, for example printing machine managers (634 .10 and 634 .15), and are not classified as managers.

Managers are in groups which can easily be related to the type of work managed:

(1) General managers (major group I) are those in both public and private sectors who determine

and influence the broad objectives of organisations and the resources to be made available for their attainment and therefore have significant responsibilities in more than one major field of activity. They usually work through other managers and with the support of professional and technical specialists and have complete control of an organisation or of divisions of a large organisation. The main emphasis of their work is on the formulation and interpretation of policy, long-term planning and important decision-taking. They are mainly top level managers and as such form a distinct group. Directors and general managers of large and medium-sized organisations are included unless they can be classified more specifically elsewhere, for example as accountants or works managers. Principals of small firms and working managers are normally excluded and classified to operational management (major group VI) or specialist occupations (major groups II to V).

(2) Operational managers (major group VI) are those who are responsible for a specific field of activity, whose prime tasks are to see that the work they control is efficiently organised and carried out. Generally therefore they need to have a good understanding of the work carried out by workers under their control. They are line managers and usually work through supervisors and/or foremen, though some work through other managers, whilst others directly control staff. Broadly speaking they comprise those middle and junior managers whose management responsibilities of controlling, planning, organising and directing work and resources outweigh their specialist responsibilities.

Operational managers are classified in two minor groups, one covering the management of industrial processing, production and transport and the other covering farm management and the management of service activities. Each minor group is subdivided into unit groups related to activities in easily identifiable groups classified elsewhere. Thus the office management occupations in unit group 281 relate to clerical occupations in major group VII.

(3) Managers of specialist activities are classified to their specialism, in the same groups as similar specialists who are not managers, rather than to managerial groups as such. Specialist managers are those in charge of a specific field of activity whose contribution is primarily intellectual and based on acquired specialist knowledge. The main emphasis of their work is maintaining the professional or technical quality of the work done, usually by specialist staff. Thus such specialist managers and their equivalents as personnel managers, management services managers, chief accountants, borough engineers, managers of engineering design or scientific research and development departments, headmasters, and editors are not classified in managerial groups but in the groups for personnel and management services specialists, accountants, civil engineers, mechanical engineers, natural science specialists, teachers and writers respectively. Whenever appropriate, unit groups for specialists contain a separate occupation for a specialist manager or his equivalent, often coded .00.

Working Principals

Working principal or working proprietor is a status rather than an occupation and therefore is not classified as such. In many cases working principals are treated as managers because they have independent responsibility, which involves the performance of managerial functions. This can apply even though they may not have supervisors under their control. Thus working principals of wholesale and retail establishments, catering and lodging establishments, and farms, for example, are classified under managerial occupations in major group VI and their existence recognised by the inclusion of the phrase "on own account or on behalf of employer" in the appropriate definitions. However, working principals of small undertakings who exercise a professional or craft function, and whose managerial role is clearly subordinate to the application of specialist skills, are classified to those skills; for example working principal accountants, bakers, and electricians are classified as accountants, bakers and electricians and not as managers.

Supervisors/Foremen

Supervisors are identified in groups which can easily be related to the type of work supervised. They are classified exclusively in unit groups with the third digit '0' in the minor group appropriate to the workers supervised. Supervisors are regarded as those whose prime function is to directly organise, control and co-ordinate the day-to-day activities of basic production and service workers. Those workers whose primary task is to carry out the work of the group but who have a subsidiary additional function of allocating work and controlling its execution (for example, those sometimes known as working foremen, leading hands or charge hands, or those workers controlling other workers in the same sphere like senior radiographers or leading draughtsmen) are classified with the workers under their control and not as supervisors/foremen.

The terms 'supervisor', 'foreman', 'charge hand' (when a supervisor), 'ganger', 'overlooker' (when a supervisor) and 'overseer' are considered to be synonymous. In the occupational definitions the term supervisor is generally used for those in immediate control of workers in major groups VII to X and foreman for those in immediate control of workers in major groups XI to XVIII.

National and Local Government officials

Civil servants and local authority officials who carry out functions which are found outside the Civil Service and Local Government are classified according to those functions; for example civil servants and local authority officials who work as scientists, surveyors, office managers, vocational trainers, machine operators, typists and messengers are classified to these occupations. A small group are top managers and classified accordingly in major group I. There are however a number of civil servants and local authority officials who have no outside counterparts because they are interpreting and implementing national and local government policies, laws and regulations. Some of these have been classified in unit groups covering related work, for example tax inspectors with tax consultants and medical officers of health with doctors. For the remainder, two residual occupations have been included in major group II, namely national government officer and local government officer (administrative and executive functions) (not elsewhere classified) (069 .20 and 069 .30).

Members of the Armed Forces

Members of the Armed Forces whose occupations have civilian counterparts are classified to those occupations, for example medical officers, aircraft pilots, maintenance fitters, cooks and drivers. Those whose occupations have no civilian counterpart, for example Infantry, RAF Regiment and Royal Marine officers, gunners, bomb disposal engineers, are classified, if officers, in managerial occupations in major group VI, or if NCOs or other ranks, in security and protective service occupations in major group IX.

Trainees

Trainees are classified according to the occupation being learned. They are given code numbers ending .98 preceded by the same three digit code numbers as corresponding trained workers. Apprentices, learners, trainees under articles, pupils and cadets are included.

Labourers

Labourers are classified as follows:

(1) Mates and labourers assisting craftsmen by performing particular tasks for them are classified

either in exclusive unit groups (eg pipe, sheet and structural metal workers' mates and labourers in unit group 776) or in the residual unit group of the minor group in which the craftsmen are classified (eg mates to carpenters (671) are classified in unit group 679).

(2) Labourers whose tasks are clearly tied to a particular process or activity are classified in the residual unit group of the minor group covering the activity or process; for example, in the metal processing minor group (71), labourers specifically assisting furnace and rolling mill teams are classified in unit group 719.

(3) Workers who may be known as labourers but who perform tasks wholly concerned with moving materials are classified in minor group 95, 'Materials moving and storing and related occupations'. Titles given to the occupations in this group reflect the work performed, for example works porter, vehicle loader, refuse collector.

(4) The majority of labourers perform tasks of a general nature and are classified in unit group 991, 'Labourers and general hands not elsewhere classified'.

NOTES ON CERTAIN OCCUPATIONAL GROUPS

The following notes give further information about some of the major groups:

Major Group III   Professional and Related Occupations in Education, Welfare and Health

Vocational and industrial trainers and instructors are included in teaching and instructing occupations. Religious occupations include only those who perform sacerdotal or similar functions closely related to religious worship. Those in holy orders performing lay functions such as teaching, nursing or librarianship are classified to those functions.

Major Group IV   Literary, Artistic and Sports Occupations

This group is composed principally of occupations in literature, the arts and sport which call for the exercise of individual talents and in many cases for creative work, as in the case of certain artists, performers and writers. It also includes workers operating television and radio broadcasting and other sound and vision equipment, who have to use some artistic judgement in their work.

Major Group V   Professional and Related Occupations in Science, Engineering, Technology and Similar Fields

Technicians who generally support specialist technologists, engineers and scientists and perform allied functions are included in the residual minor group of this major group. The distinction between technological, engineering and scientific specialist occupations on the one hand and technical supporting occupations on the other is not based on qualifications but on the nature of the work performed. In practice the distinction will often fall between those with graduate and those with non-graduate qualifications, although there are many non-graduates who perform technological, engineering and scientific functions and graduates who perform technical supporting functions as defined in CODOT. Two levels of technical supporting occupations in engineering (technician engineer and engineering technician) are becoming increasingly recognised, but separate occupations are not provided for them because a sufficiently valid demarcation has not yet emerged in terms of work performed.

INTRODUCTION

Major Group VIII   Selling Occupations

This group covers occupations in the selling of goods, property and services of all kinds and therefore excludes shop cashiers who are in clerical occupations in major group VII. It also excludes shop managers who are classified as managers in major group VI, and company sales managers, buyers and manufacturers agents who are classified as specialists in major group II. Barmen, waiters and similar workers who are considered to be performing a catering rather than a selling function, are also excluded and classified in major group X.

Major Groups XII, XIII and XIV   Materials Processing, Making and Repairing Occupations

These three major groups cover processing and production occupations. In forming these three major groups, two broad distinctions have been drawn:

(a) between metal and electrical materials and products on the one hand and other materials and products on the other; and

(b) in the 'other materials and products' area, between processing occupations on the one hand and making and repairing occupations on the other.

In some areas the processing of raw materials is so inextricably linked with the preparing and making of products that strict application of the distinction between processing and making and repairing has not been practicable; for example, tobacco processors and tobacco product makers are grouped together.

In general the relationship between the occupations included in a particular minor group is reflected in such factors as processing or working similar materials (eg fibres, tobacco, leather, wood) or carrying out similar processes (in printing occupations) or applying similar skills and knowledge (as in electronic and electrical equipment making, electrical wiring). Inevitably such grouping tends to give this part of the classification a quasi-industrial aspect because particular industries have occupations specific to them.

Occupations which involve the working of alternative materials are classified to the same occupations as the original material, provided that both materials are worked in the same way; for example, plastics worked as metal are treated as metal; plastic material worked as leather for footwear is treated as leather.

In major group XII 'Materials processing occupations (excluding metal)', unit groups have been provided in most minor groups for occupations involving common operations such as heat treating, crushing, mixing and filtering. In chemical, gas and petroleum processing however, these operations are becoming increasingly merged into a continuous process, so that it has not been meaningful to provide separate unit groups for such occupations, although separate occupations have been provided for both batch and continuous process workers.

In major group XIII 'Making and repairing occupations (excluding metal and electrical)', some of the minor groups correspond to minor groups in the materials processing major group XII. For example leather workers (66) produce finished articles from the materials processed by hide, skin and pelt processors (53) and similarly with glass (61 and 59), textiles (65 and 54), paper (64 and 58) and rubber and plastics (68 and 59).

In major group XIV 'Processing, making, repairing and related occupations (metal and electrical)', separate minor groups are provided for production fitting occupations and for installing, maintaining and repairing occupations. In the metal production fitting groups, fitter-assemblers working to close tolerances (engineering production fitters (733)) are distinguished from other fitter-assemblers (metal working production fitters (734)). These two groups of fitter-assemblers are themselves distinguished from the repetitive assemblers who are classified in major group XV.

Major Group XVI   Construction, Mining and Related Occupations NEC

This is a major group for occupations in construction and mining which are not classified elsewhere. Most construction industry occupations are in this group—bricklayers, roofers, terrazzo and tile workers, plasterers, glaziers, concrete erectors, road and rail track makers—but others not exclusive to construction are classified elsewhere, including carpenters and joiners (67), electricians (76), plumbers and steel erectors (77) and painters (81).

The principal underground mining occupations are also classified in this major group but occupations not exclusive to underground mining are classified elsewhere (eg electricians (76), locomotive drivers (92), materials handling equipment operators (94)).

USING CODOT TO ASSIST DEPLOYMENT OF WORKERS

CODOT'S structure of groups of occupations linked by similarity of work performed makes it a useful document for deployment of workers. This is especially true of the unit group, which generally provides a convenient collection of occupations for consideration of alternative fields for deployment. Other guidance on occupations which are linked and which could therefore be considered for deployment is given by the following means:

(1) direct cross reference in the 'how items' from one occupation to another.

(2) reference in the 'may items' to other occupations whose functions may be performed in full or part by workers in that occupation.

(3) 'see items' which indicate a work-performed connection between occupations.

(4) 'exclusions', since excluded occupations usually have some connection with the group from which they are excluded.

Other assistance towards deployment is provided by additional factors.

NOTES ON INDEX OF TITLES

With a few exceptions all titles used in the occupational definitions are listed in alphabetical sequence in the index which contains more than 10,000 titles. The titles are arranged under the functional word (ie the word most nearly describing the work performed); for example cost accountant is indexed under accountant, monumental mason under mason and drilling machine operator under operator. The following are not regarded as functional words for indexing purposes:

Assistant	Extra	Lad	Orderly
Auxiliary	Girl	Man	Specialist
Boy	Hand	Mate	Woman
Executive	Helper	Officer	Worker

The index is arranged in alphabetical order of complete words. Hyphenated words are regarded as single words. Titles comprising two words or phrases joined by 'and' immediately follow entries relating to the first word or phrase.

Functional (or indexing) words alone are usually insufficient for identification purposes and qualifying terms are therefore added where necessary. When considered appropriate, a title having more than one word has been indexed in its inverted as well as its usual form.

Where two or more titles are used for similar jobs in a particular occupation and the titles are similar in form, only one is used in the index. Thus although a receptionist at one establishment might be called a reception desk clerk at another, only receptionist has been indexed. Specialisations—of process, material or machine—are often reflected in job titles. The majority of these specialist titles are not in the index but such omissions should not cause difficulty as the functional part of the title is indexed. Thus a broker is indexed but not every specialist commodity broker.

With a few exceptions, the titles of minor and unit groups are included in the index and are indicated by an asterisk (*) and a dagger (†) respectively. Residual occupations have not been indexed, but the functional titles have been included. Titles of individual occupations included in those unit groups with a chart have not been indexed but the functional titles have been included. These are sufficiently explicit to guide the user to the correct chart for individual occupation.

Occupational numbers should not be decided merely by reference to titles in the index. The aim of the index is to lead the user to the appropriate classification in Volumes II or III.

NOTES ON GLOSSARY

A glossary of terms is provided at the end of this Volume. It includes only those terms used in the classification whose meaning is not clear from the context and which are not defined in the Concise Oxford Dictionary.

STRUCTURE OF THE CLASSIFICATION

Major, Minor and Unit Groups

MANAGERIAL OCCUPATIONS (GENERAL MANAGEMENT)

00 Managerial Occupations (General Management)
  1 Ministers of the Crown, Members of Parliament and General Administrators (National and Local Government)
  2 Directors and Managers (General Management) (Other than National and Local Government)

II PROFESSIONAL AND RELATED OCCUPATIONS SUPPORTING MANAGEMENT AND ADMINISTRATION

02 Legal Service and Related Occupations
  1 Judges and Officers of the Court
  2 Counsel and Solicitors
  3 Adjudicators NEC
  9 Legal Service and Related Occupations NEC

03 Company Secretarial, Accounting, Financial and Insurance Specialist Occupations (Excluding Clerical)
  1 Company and Similar Executive Secretaries
  2 Accountants
  3 Estimating, Valuing and Assessing Occupations
  4 Finance, Investment and Insurance Specialist Occupations
  9 Company Secretarial, Accounting, Financial and Insurance Specialist Occupations (Excluding Clerical) NEC

04 Personnel and Management Services Specialist Occupations
  1 Personnel Management and Industrial Relations Specialist Occupations
  2 Operational Research, Organisation and Methods, Work Study and Related Specialist Occupations
  3 Economic, Statistical and Actuarial Specialist Occupations
  4 Automatic Data Processing (ADP) Planning and Programming Occupations
  9 Personnel and Management Services Specialist Occupations NEC

05 Marketing, Advertising and Public Relations Specialist Occupations
  1 Marketing, Advertising and Public Relations Specialist Occupations

06 Professional and Related Occupations Supporting Management and Administration NEC
  1 Purchasing and Procurement Managers and Executives
  2 Property and Estate Management Occupations
  3 Library, Records, Information and Related Specialist Occupations
  4 Inspectors (Statutory and Similar Requirements)
  9 Other Professional and Related Occupations Supporting Management and Administration

CO1—B

STRUCTURE

III PROFESSIONAL AND RELATED OCCUPATIONS IN EDUCATION, WELFARE AND HEALTH

09 Teaching and Instructing Occupations
  1 Teaching Occupations (University Education)
  2 Teaching Occupations (Teacher Training)
  3 Teaching Occupations (Further Education) (Technical, Vocational and Related)
  4 Teaching Occupations (Secondary Education)
  5 Teaching Occupations (Primary Education)
  6 Teaching Occupations (Pre-Primary Education)
  7 Teaching Occupations (Special Education)
  8 Vocational Training Occupations
  9 Teaching and Instructing Occupations NEC

10 Social Science, Welfare and Religious Occupations
  1 Social Scientists and Related Occupations
  2 Welfare Occupations
  3 Religious Occupations
  9 Social Science, Welfare and Religious Occupations NEC

11 Health Diagnosing and Treating Occupations
  1 Medical Practitioners
  2 Dental Practitioners
  3 Nursing Occupations
  4 Pharmacists
  5 Medical Radiographers
  6 Opticians
  7 Physio-, Occupational, Speech and Related Therapists
  9 Health Diagnosing and Treating Occupations NEC

12 Animal Health Occupations
  1 Veterinarians
  9 Animal Health Occupations NEC

IV LITERARY, ARTISTIC AND SPORTS OCCUPATIONS

15 Literary Occupations
  1 Editors, Writers, Journalists and Related Literary Occupations
  9 Literary Occupations NEC

16 Artists, Sculptors and Industrial Designers
  1 Artists and Sculptors
  2 Industrial Designers

17 Performing, Audio and Visual Arts Occupations NEC
  1 Directors, Producers, Managers and Related Occupations (Performing, Audio and Visual Arts)
  2 Musical Composers and Choreographers
  3 Performers (Entertainment)
  4 Photographers and Cameramen
  5 Sound and Vision Equipment Operators (Artistic) (Excluding Cameramen)
  9 Other Performing, Audio and Visual Arts Occupations

18 Professional Sportsmen, Coaches and Sports Officials
  1 Professional Sportsmen, Coaches and Sports Officials

V PROFESSIONAL AND RELATED OCCUPATIONS IN SCIENCE, ENGINEERING, TECHNOLOGY AND SIMILAR FIELDS

21 Natural Sciences Research, Development, Technical Advisory, Consultancy and Related Occupations
    1 Biological Scientists (Research, Development, Technical Advisory, Consultancy nd Related Work)
    2 Chemical Scientists (Research, Development, Analysis, Technical Advisory, Consultancy and Related Work)
    3 Physical Scientists (Research, Development, Technical Advisory, Consultancy and Related Work)
    4 Geological Scientists (Research, Development, Technical Advisory, Consultancy and Related Work)
    5 Mathematicians
    9 Natural Sciences Research, Development, Technical Advisory, Consultancy and Related Occupations NEC

22 Engineering Research and Development, Design, Feasibility Studies, Applications, Liaison, Consultancy and Related Occupations
    1 Civil and Structural Engineering, Research and Development, Design, Feasibility Studies, Liaison, Consultancy and Related Occupations
    2 Mining, Quarrying and Drilling Engineers
    3 Mechanical Engineering Research and Development, Design, Feasibility Studies, Applications, Liaison, Consultancy and Related Occupations
    4 Electrical and Electronic Engineering Research and Development, Design, Feasibility Studies, Applications, Liaison, Consultancy and Related Occupations
    5 Chemical Engineering Research and Development, Design, Feasibility Studies, Applications, Liaison, Consultancy and Related Occupations
    6 Production Engineers
    9 Engineering Research and Development, Design, Feasibility Studies, Applications, Liaison, Consultancy and Related Occupations NEC

23 Technological (Excluding Engineering) Research and Development, Design, Feasibility Studies, Applications, Liaison, Consultancy and Related Occupations
    1 Technological (Excluding Engineering) Research and Development, Design, Feasibility Studies, Applications, Liaison, Consultancy and Related Occupations

24 Aircraft and Ships' Officers and Related Occupations
    1 Flight Deck Officers
    2 Air Traffic Planning and Controlling Occupations
    3 Masters, Deck Officers and Pilots (Ship)
    4 Engineer and Radio Officers (Ship)
    9 Aircraft and Ships' Officers and Related Occupations NEC

25 Professional and Related Occupations in Science, Engineering, Technology and Similar Fields NEC
    1 Town Planners and Architects
    2 Surveyors
    3 Draughtsmen
    4 Laboratory Technicians and Similar Scientific Supporting Occupations
    5 Architectural, Constructional and Related Technical Supporting Occupations NEC
    6 Engineering (Excluding Architectural, Constructional and Related) Technical Supporting Occupations NEC
    9 Other Professional and Related Occupations in Science, Engineering, Technology and Similar Fields

STRUCTURE

VI MANAGERIAL OCCUPATIONS (EXCLUDING GENERAL MANAGEMENT)

27 Managerial Occupations (Industrial Operations)
  1 Managerial Occupations (Production Process) (Metal and Electrical)
  2 Managerial Occupations (Production Process) (Excluding Metal and Electrical)
  3 Managerial Occupations (Engineering Maintenance)
  4 Managerial Occupations (Construction)
  5 Managerial Occupations (Mining, Quarrying and Well Drilling)
  6 Managerial Occupations (Production and Supply of Gas, Water and Electricity)
  7 Managerial Occupations (Transport Operating, Warehousing and Materials Handling)
  9 Managerial Occupations (Industrial Operations) NEC

28 Managerial Occupations (Services and NEC)
  1 Managerial Occupations (Office)
  2 Managerial Occupations (Wholesale Distributive Trade)
  3 Managerial Occupations (Retail Distributive Trade)
  4 Managerial Occupations (Catering, Hotels and Public Houses)
  5 Managerial Occupations (Recreation and Amenity Services)
  6 Managerial Occupations (Farming, Fishing and Related)
  7 Officers (Armed Forces) NEC
  8 Managerial Occupations (Police, Fire Fighting and Related Protective Services)
  9 Managerial Occupations (Administration and NEC)

VII CLERICAL AND RELATED OCCUPATIONS

31 Clerical Occupations
  0 Supervisors (Clerical Occupations)
  1 Costing and Accounting Clerical Occupations
  2 Cash Handling Clerical Occupations
  3 Finance, Investment and Insurance Clerical Occupations
  4 Production and Materials Controlling Clerical Occupations
  5 Shipment and Travel Arranging Clerical Occupations
  6 Record Keeping and Library Clerical Occupations
  9 General Clerical Occupations and Clerical Occupations NEC

32 Shorthand, Typewriting and Related Secretarial Occupations
  0 Supervisors (Shorthand, Typewriting and Related Secretarial Occupations)
  1 Shorthand Writing and Related Occupations
  2 Typewriting Occupations

33 Office Machine Operating Occupations (Excluding Telecommunications)
  0 Supervisors (Office Machine Operating Occupations (Excluding Telecommunications))
  1 Accounting and Calculating Machine Operators
  2 Automatic Data Processing Equipment Operating Occupations
  3 Key Punch Operating Occupations
  4 Document Reproducing Machine Operating Occupations
  9 Office Machine Operating Occupations (Excluding Telecommunications) NEC

34 Telecommunications Operating and Mail Distributing Occupations
  0 Supervisors (Telecommunications Operating and Mail Distributing Occupations)
  1 Telephone Operators
  2 Radio and Telegraphic Equipment Operating Occupations
  3 Mail, Parcel and Message Distributing Occupations

VIII SELLING OCCUPATIONS

36 Selling Occupations (Distributive Trade)
- 0 Supervisors (Selling Occupations (Distributive Trade))
- 1 Salesmen and Shop Assistants
- 2 Roundsmen
- 3 Street Trading Occupations
- 9 Selling Occupations (Distributive Trade) NEC

37 Sales Representatives, Agents and Related Occupations
- 1 Technical Sales Representatives
- 2 Sales Representatives (Wholesale Goods)
- 3 Sales Representatives (Property and Services)
- 9 Sales Representatives, Agents and Related Occupations NEC

IX SECURITY AND PROTECTIVE SERVICE OCCUPATIONS

40 Armed Forces Occupations NEC
- 0 Warrant Officers, Petty Officers and Other Non-Commissioned Officers NEC
- 1 Other Ranks, Armed Forces NEC

41 Police, Fire Fighting and Related Protective Service Occupations
- 0 Sergeants and Other Supervisors (Police, Fire Fighting and Related Protective Service Occupations)
- 1 Policemen (Statutory Forces)
- 2 Fire Fighting, Fire Prevention and Salvage Occupations
- 9 Police, Fire Fighting and Related Protective Service Occupations NEC

X CATERING, CLEANING, HAIRDRESSING AND OTHER PERSONAL SERVICE OCCUPATIONS

43 Food and Beverage Preparing, Serving and Related Occupations
- 0 Supervisors (Food and Beverage Preparing, Serving and Related Occupations)
- 1 Cooks (Catering Services)
- 2 Waiters and Waitresses
- 3 Barmen, Barmaids and Bar Stewards
- 4 Food and Beverage Dispensers and Counter Hands (Catering Services)
- 5 Kitchen and Dining Room Hands
- 9 Food and Beverage Preparing, Serving and Related Occupations NEC

44 Housekeepers, Personal Service Attendants and Related Occupations (Excluding Cleaners)
- 0 Supervisors (Housekeepers, Personal Service Attendants and Related Occupations (Excluding Cleaners))
- 1 Housekeepers, Maids and Related Personal Service Occupations
- 2 Stewards and Attendants (Travel and Transport Services)
- 3 Ward Orderlies and Medical Attendants
- 9 Porters and Attendants and Housekeepers and Related Personal Service Occupations NEC

45 Caretaking, Cleaning and Attending Occupations (Premises and Property)
- 0 Supervisors and Foremen (Caretaking, Cleaning and Attending Occupations (Premises and Property))
- 1 Caretakers
- 2 Cleaners
- 3 Stationmen (Railway)
- 9 Attendants (Premises and Property) NEC

46 Laundering, Dry Cleaning and Pressing Occupations
- 0 Supervisors (Laundering, Dry Cleaning and Pressing Occupations)
- 1 Laundering, Dry Cleaning and Pressing Occupations

47 Hairdressing and Miscellaneous Service Occupations
    0   Supervisors (Hairdressing and Miscellaneous Services Occupations)
    1   Hairdressing and Beauty Treatment Occupations
    2   Burial and Related Service Occupations
    9   Miscellaneous Service Occupations NEC

XI FARMING, FISHING AND RELATED OCCUPATIONS

50 Farming, Horticultural, Forestry and Related Occupations
    0   Foremen (Farming, Horticultural, Forestry and Related Occupations)
    1   Farm Workers (Arable and Mixed Farming)
    2   Animal Tending and Breeding Occupations
    3   Horticultural Workers
    4   Gardeners and Groundsmen
    5   Agricultural Machinery Operators
    6   Tree Cultivating and Harvesting Occupations
    9   Farming, Horticultural, Forestry and Related Occupations NEC

51 Fishing and Related Occupations
    0   Supervisors and Mates (Fishing and Related Occupations)
    1   Fishermen
    9   Fishing and Related Occupations NEC

XII MATERIALS PROCESSING OCCUPATIONS (EXCLUDING METAL)

53 Hide Skin and Pelt Processing Occupations
    0   Foremen (Hide Skin and Pelt Processing Occupations)
    1   Hide Skin and Pelt Processing Occupations

54 Fibre and Textile Processing and Fabric Making Occupations
    0   Foremen (Fibre and Textile Processing and Fabric Making Occupations)
    1   Fibre Preparing Occupations
    2   Textile Spinning, Doubling, Twisting and Winding Occupations
    3   Warp Preparing Occupations
    4   Textile Weaving Occupations
    5   Knitting Occupations
    6   Textile Bleaching, Dyeing, Finishing and Other Treating Occupations
    7   Textile Repairing Occupations
    8   Braid, Plait, Line and Fibre Rope Making Occupations
    9   Fibre and Textile Processing and Fabric Making Occupations NEC

55 Tobacco Processing and Products Making Occupations
    0   Foremen (Tobacco Processing and Products Making Occupations)
    1   Tobacco Processing and Products Making Occupations

56 Chemical, Gas and Petroleum Processing Plant Operating Occupations
    0   Supervisors (Chemical, Gas and Petroleum Processing Plant Operating Occupations)
    1   Chemical, Gas and Petroleum Processing Plant Operating Occupations

57 Food and Drink Processing Occupations

    0 Foremen (Food and Drink Processing Occupations)
    1 Bakers and Flour Confectioners
    2 Meat, Fish and Poultry Slaughtering and Preparing Occupations
    3 Cooking, Freezing and Other Heat Treating Occupations (Food and Drink Processing)
    4 Crushing, Milling, Mixing and Blending Occupations (Food and Drink Processing)
    5 Filtering, Straining and Other Separating Occupations (Food and Drink Processing)
    6 Plant and Machine Operating Occupations (Food and Drink Processing) NEC
    9 Food and Drink Processing Occupations NEC

58 Wood Processing and Paper, Paperboard and Leatherboard Making Occupations

    0 Foremen (Wood Processing and Paper, Paperboard and Leatherboard Making Occupations)
    1 Heat Treating Occupations (Wood Processing and Paper, Paperboard and Leatherboard Making)
    2 Crushing, Milling, Mixing and Blending Occupations (Wood Processing and Paper, Paperboard and Leatherboard Making)
    3 Filtering, Straining and Other Separating Occupations (Wood Processing and Paper, Paperboard and Leatherboard Making)
    4 Plant and Machine Operating Occupations (Wood Processing and Paper, Paperboard and Leatherboard Making) NEC
    9 Wood Processing and Paper, Paperboard and Leatherboard Making Occupations NEC

59 Materials Processing Occupations NEC

    0 Foremen (Materials Processing Occupations NEC)
    1 Heat Treating Occupations NEC
    2 Crushing, Milling, Mixing and Blending Occupations NEC
    3 Filtering, Straining and Other Mechanical Separating Occupations NEC
    4 Plant and Machine Operating Occupations (Materials Processing) NEC
    9 Other Materials Processing Occupations

XIII MAKING AND REPAIRING OCCUPATIONS (EXCLUDING METAL AND ELECTRICAL)

61 Glass Working Occupations

    0 Foremen (Glass Working Occupations)
    1 Glass Shaping and Forming Occupations (Hand) (Excluding Optical Glass)
    2 Glass Shaping and Forming Occupations (Machine) (Excluding Optical Glass)
    3 Optical Glass Shaping, Forming and Finishing Occupations
    4 Glass Finishing Occupations (Excluding Optical Glass and Painting)
    9 Glass Working Occupations NEC

62 Clay and Stone Working Occupations

    0 Foremen (Clay and Stone Working Occupations)
    1 Ceramic Goods Forming Occupations
    2 Ceramic Goods Finishing Occupations (Excluding Glazers and Decorators)
    3 Concrete, Asbestos-Cement, Abrasive Stone and Related Products Making Occupations
    4 Stone Cutting, Shaping and Polishing Occupations
    9 Clay and Stone Working Occupations NEC

63 Printing, Photographic Processing and Related Occupations

    0 Foremen (Printing, Photographic Processing and Related Occupations)
    1 Printers (General)
    2 Composing and Typesetting Occupations
    3 Printing Plate and Cylinder Preparing Occupations (Excluding Metal Engraving)
    4 Printing Machine Operators (Excluding Screen and Block Printing)
    5 Screen and Block Printing Occupations
    6 Photographic Processing and Related Occupations
    9 Printing, Photographic Processing and Related Occupations NEC

64 Bookbinding, Paper Working and Paperboard Products Making Occupations

    0 Foremen (Bookbinding, Paper Working and Paperboard Products Making Occupations)
    1 Bookbinding Occupations
    2 Paper Working and Paperboard Products Making Occupations

STRUCTURE

65 Textile Materials Working Occupations
- 0 Foremen (Textile Materials Working Occupations)
- 1 Tailors
- 2 Dressmakers and Makers Throughout of Other Light Clothing
- 3 Upholsterers, Mattress Makers and Related Occupations
- 4 Milliners
- 5 Fur Garment Cutting and Shaping Occupations
- 6 Pattern Makers, Markers and Cutters (Garments, Upholstery and Related Products)
- 7 Sewing and Embroidering Occupations (Hand) (Garments, Upholstery and Related Products)
- 8 Sewing and Embroidering Occupations (Machine) (Garments, Upholstery and Related Products)
- 9 Textile Materials Working Occupations NEC

66 Leather Working Occupations
- 0 Foremen (Leather Working Occupations)
- 1 Boot and Shoe Making (Bespoke and Surgical) Occupations
- 2 Leather Cutting Occupations
- 3 Lasting Occupations (Footwear)
- 4 Leather Goods Makers and Repairers (Excluding Boots and Shoes)
- 5 Leather Sewing and Stitching Occupations
- 6 Boot and Shoe Repairers
- 9 Leather Working Occupations NEC

67 Woodworking Occupations
- 0 Foremen (Woodworking Occupations)
- 1 Carpenters, and Carpenters and Joiners (Structural Woodworking)
- 2 Cabinet Makers
- 3 Wood Fitting and Joinery Occupations (Excluding Structural Woodworking and Cabinet Makers)
- 4 Wood Sawing and Veneer Cutting Occupations
- 5 Setters and Setter-Operators (Woodworking Machines)
- 6 Operators and Minders (Woodworking Machines)
- 7 Pattern Makers (Moulds)
- 9 Woodworking Occupations NEC

68 Rubber and Plastics Working Occupations
- 0 Foremen (Rubber and Plastics Working Occupations)
- 1 Rubber and Plastics Working Occupations

69 Making and Repairing Occupations NEC
- 0 Foremen (Making and Repairing Occupations NEC)
- 1 Musical Instrument Making and Repairing Occupations NEC
- 2 Surgical Appliance Makers
- 9 Other Making and Repairing Occupations

XIV PROCESSING, MAKING, REPAIRING AND RELATED OCCUPATIONS (METAL AND ELECTRICAL)

71 Metal Processing, Forming and Treating Occupations
- 0 Foremen (Metal Processing, Forming and Treating Occupations)
- 1 Furnace Operating Occupations (Metal Processing)
- 2 Rolling, Extruding and Drawing Occupations (Metal Processing)
- 3 Moulders, Coremakers and Casters (Metal Processing)
- 4 Forging Occupations
- 5 Metal Plating and Coating Occupations
- 6 Metal Annealing and Tempering Occupations
- 9 Metal Processing, Forming and Treating Occupations NEC

72 Machining and Related Occupations (Engineering and Metal Goods Making)
0 Foremen (Machining and Related Occupations (Engineering and Metal Goods Making))
1 Press, Machine Tool and Other Metal Working Machine Setters
2 Machine Tool Setter-Operators (Metal Working)
3 Machine Tool Operators (Metal Working)
4 Press and Stamping Machine Operators (Metal Working)
5 Automatic Machine Attendants (Metal Working)
6 Fettling, Grinding (Excluding Machine Tool) and Polishing Occupations (Metal)
9 Machining and Related Occupations (Engineering and Metal Goods Making) NEC

73 Production Fitting (Metal) and Related Occupations
0 Foremen (Production Fitting (Metal) and Related Occupations)
1 Toolmakers, Tool Fitters and Markers-Out
2 Precision Instrument Making Occupations
3 Other Engineering Production Fitters (Excluding Electrical)
4 Other Metal Working Production Fitters
9 Production Fitting (Metal) and Related Occupations NEC

74 Installing, Maintaining and Repairing Occupations (Machines, Instruments and Related Mechanical Equipment)
0 Foremen (Installing, Maintaining and Repairing Occupations (Machines, Instruments and Related Mechanical Equipment))
1 Installation and Maintenance Fitters and Fitter-Mechanics (Plant, Industrial Engines and Machinery and Other Mechanical Equipment)
2 Fitter-Mechanics (Motor Vehicles)
3 Maintenance Fitters and Fitter-Mechanics (Aircraft Engines)
4 Precision Instrument Maintaining and Repairing Occupations
5 Office Machinery Maintaining and Repairing Occupations (Mechanical)
6 Servicing, Oiling, Greasing and Related Occupations (Mechanical)
9 Installing, Maintaining and Repairing Occupations (Machines, Instruments and Related Mechanical Equipment) NEC

75 Production Fitting and Wiring Occupations (Electrical and Electronic)
0 Foremen (Production Fitting and Wiring Occupations (Electrical and Electronic))
1 Production Fitters (Electrical and Electronic)
2 Electricians (Production)
9 Production Fitting and Wiring Occupations (Electrical and Electronic) NEC

76 Installing, Maintaining and Repairing Occupations (Electrical and Electronic)
0 Foremen (Installing, Maintaining and Repairing Occupations (Electrical and Electronic))
1 Electricians (Installation, Maintenance and Repair) (Plant, Machinery and Other Equipment)
2 Electricians (Installation, Maintenance and Repair) (Premises and Ships)
3 Installing, Maintaining and Repairing Occupations (Electronic and Related Equipment)
4 Linesmen and Cable Jointers
9 Installing, Maintaining and Repairing Occupations (Electrical and Electronic) NEC

77 Pipe, Sheet and Structural Metal Working and Related Occupations
0 Foremen (Pipe, Sheet and Structural Metal Working and Related Occupations)
1 Plumbing, Heating and Ventilating and Pipe Fitting Occupations
2 Sheet Metal Working Occupations
3 Metal Plate Working and Riveting Occupations
4 Steel Erecting and Rigging and Cable Splicing Occupations
5 Welding and Flame Cutting Occupations (Metal)
6 Pipe, Sheet and Structural Metal Workers' Mates and Labourers
9 Pipe, Sheet and Structural Metal Working and Related Occupations NEC

79 Processing, Making, Repairing and Related Occupations (Metal and Electrical) NEC
- 0 Foremen (Processing, Making, Repairing and Related Occupations (Metal and Electrical) NEC)
- 1 Goldsmiths, Silversmiths, Precious Stone Working and Related Occupations
- 2 Metal Engraving Occupations
- 3 Vehicle Body Builders and Aircraft Finishers
- 9 Other Processing, Making, Repairing and Related Occupations (Metal and Electrical)

XV PAINTING, REPETITIVE ASSEMBLING, PRODUCT INSPECTING, PACKAGING AND RELATED OCCUPATIONS

81 Painting and Related Coating Occupations
- 0 Foremen (Painting and Related Coating Occupations)
- 1 Painting and Decorating Occupations (Structures)
- 2 Painting and Related Coating Occupations (Brush) (Excluding Structures)
- 3 Painting and Related Coating Occupations (Spray) (Excluding Structures)
- 4 Painting and Related Coating Occupations (Dip)
- 5 Wood Staining, Waxing and French Polishing Occupations (Hand)
- 9 Painting and Related Coating Occupations NEC

82 Product Assembling Occupations (Repetitive)
- 0 Foremen (Product Assembling Occupations (Repetitive))
- 1 Product Assembling Occupations (Repetitive)

83 Product Inspecting, Examining, Sorting, Grading and Measuring Occupations (Excluding Laboratory Technicians)
- 0 Foremen (Product Inspecting, Examining, Sorting, Grading and Measuring Occupations (Excluding Laboratory Technicians))
- 1 Inspecting and Testing Occupations (Metal and Electrical Engineering)
- 2 Examining, Viewing and Checking Occupations (Metal and Electrical Engineering)
- 3 Examining, Viewing and Checking Occupations (Excluding Metal and Electrical Engineering)
- 4 Sorting and Grading Occupations
- 5 Weighing and Measuring Occupations
- 9 Product Inspecting, Examining, Sorting, Grading and Measuring Occupations (Excluding Laboratory Technicians) NEC

84 Packaging, Labelling and Related Occupations
- 0 Foremen (Packaging, Labelling and Related Occupations)
- 1 Packaging, Labelling and Related Occupations (Hand)
- 2 Packaging and Labelling Occupations (Machine)

XVI CONSTRUCTION, MINING AND RELATED OCCUPATIONS NEC

86 Construction and Related Occupations NEC
- 0 Foremen (Construction and Related Occupations NEC)
- 1 Bricklaying and Stone Setting Occupations
- 2 Plastering Occupations
- 3 Terrazzo Working and Tile Setting Occupations
- 4 Roofing Occupations
- 5 Glazing Occupations
- 6 Road and Railway Track Making and Repairing Occupations (Excluding Machine Operating)
- 7 Concrete Erecting Occupations
- 8 Building and Civil Engineering Craftsmen's Mates and Labourers NEC
- 9 Other Construction and Related Occupations

87 Mining, Quarrying, Well Drilling and Related Occupations NEC
- 0 Foremen (Mining, Quarrying, Well Drilling and Related Occupations NEC)
- 1 Drilling and Shotfiring Occupations
- 2 Tunnelling Occupations
- 3 Underground Coalmining Occupations NEC
- 9 Other Mining, Quarrying, Well Drilling and Related Occupations

XVII TRANSPORT OPERATING, MATERIALS MOVING AND STORING AND RELATED OCCUPATIONS

91 Water Transport Operating Occupations
- 0 Foremen (Water Transport Operating Occupations)
- 1 Deck and Engine Room Ratings
- 9 Water Transport Operating Occupations NEC

92 Rail Transport Operating Occupations
- 0 Foremen and Inspectors (Rail Transport Operating Occupations)
- 1 Drivers and Secondmen (Rail Transport)
- 2 Guards (Rail Transport)
- 3 Traffic Controlling Occupations (Rail Transport)

93 Road Transport Operating Occupations
- 0 Foremen and Inspectors (Road Transport Operating Occupations)
- 1 Omnibus and Coach Drivers
- 2 Heavy Goods Vehicle Drivers
- 3 Other Motor Vehicle Drivers
- 4 Conductors (Road Transport)
- 5 Drivers' Mates (Road Transport)
- 9 Road Transport Operating Occupations NEC

94 Civil Engineering and Materials Handling Equipment Operating Occupations
- 0 Foremen (Civil Engineering and Materials Handling Equipment Operating Occupations)
- 1 Earth Moving and Civil Engineering Equipment Operating Occupations
- 2 Crane, Hoist and other Materials Handling Equipment Operating Occupations
- 9 Civil Engineering and Materials Handling Equipment Operating Occupations NEC

95 Transport Operating, Materials Moving and Storing and Related Occupations NEC
- 0 Foremen (Transport Operating, Materials Moving and Storing and Related Occupations NEC)
- 1 Storekeepers, Warehousemen
- 2 Stevedores, Dockers and Related Occupations
- 9 Other Transport Operating, Materials Moving and Storing and Related Occupations

XVIII MISCELLANEOUS OCCUPATIONS

97 Machinery, Plant and Equipment Operating Occupations NEC
- 0 Foremen (Machinery, Plant and Equipment Operating Occupations NEC)
- 1 Boiler and Power Generating Machinery Operating Occupations
- 2 Valvemen, Turncocks and Related Occupations
- 3 Electricity Switchboard Attending Occupations
- 9 Other Machinery, Plant and Equipment Operating Occupations

99 Miscellaneous Occupations NEC
- 0 Supervisors and Foremen NEC
- 1 Labourers and General Hands NEC
- 9 Other Occupations

CLASSIFIED LIST OF TITLES & CODES

Major Group I MANAGERIAL OCCUPATIONS (GENERAL MANAGEMENT)

00 Managerial Occupations (General Management)

001 Ministers of the Crown, Members of Parliament and General Administrators (National and Local Government)
001.10 Minister of the Crown
001.20 Member of Parliament
001.30 General administrator (national government)
001.40 General administrator (local government)
001.99 Other general administrators (national and local government)

002 Directors and Managers (General Management) (Other than National and Local Government)
002.00 Manager (general management) (unspecified)
002.05 Company director (non-executive)
002.10 General manager (agriculture, forestry, fishing or related)
002.15 General manager (mining, drilling, refining or related)
002.20 General manager (manufacturing)
002.25 General manager (construction)
002.30 General manager (utility services)
002.35 General manager (transportation, communication, storage)
002.40 General manager (distribution)
002.45 General manager (financial, business, administrative services)
002.50 General manager (technical and scientific services)
002.55 General manager (literary, artistic, cultural, recreational and related activities)
002.60 General manager (hotel and catering)
002.65 General manager (employers' association, professional body or similar organisation)
002.99 Other general managers

Major Group II PROFESSIONAL AND RELATED OCCUPATIONS SUPPORTING MANAGEMENT AND ADMINISTRATION

02 Legal Service and Related Occupations

021 Judges and Officers of the Court
021.10 Judge
021.20 Officer of the Court

022 Counsel and Solicitors
022.10 Counsel (practising in courts)
022.20 Solicitor (public practice)
022.30 Parliamentary counsel
022.40 Parliamentary agent
022.98 Trainee
022.99 Other counsel and solicitors

023 Adjudicators Not Elsewhere Classified
023.10 Housing and planning inspector
023.20 Adjudicator (national insurance regulations)
023.30 Chairman (appeals tribunal or similar body), Member (appeals tribunal or similar body)
023.40 Chairman (court, committee or commission of inquiry), Member (court, committee or commission of inquiry)
023.99 Other adjudicators not elsewhere classified

029 Legal Service and Related Occupations Not Elsewhere Classified
029.10 Barrister's clerk
029.20 Legal executive, Solicitor's managing clerk
029.98 Trainee
029.99 Other legal service and related occupations not elsewhere classified

03 Company Secretarial, Accounting, Financial and Insurance Specialist Occupations (Excluding Clerical)

031 Company and Similar Executive Secretaries
031.10 Company secretary
031.20 Town clerk
031.30 General secretary (trade union)
031.40 Secretary (trade association or similar organisation)
031.50 Secretary (professional body or similar organisation)

031.60 Secretary (charitable organisation)
031.98 Trainee
031.99 Other executive secretaries

032 Accountants

032.00 Manager
032.10 Accountant
032.20 Cost accountant
032.98 Trainee
032.99 Other accountants

033 Estimating, Valuing and Assessing Occupations

033.00 Manager
033.10 Estimator (building, civil engineering)
033.20 Estimator (mechanical engineering)
033.30 Estimator (electrical engineering)
033.40 Estimator (electronic engineering)
033.50 Valuer
033.60 Insurance assessor
033.70 Average adjuster
033.98 Trainee
033.99 Other estimating, valuing and assessing occupations

034 Finance, Investment and Insurance Specialist Occupations

034.05 Stockbroker
034.10 Stockjobber
034.15 Authorised clerk (Stock Exchange)
034.20 Licensed broker (securities)
034.25 Bill broker
034.30 Investment adviser
034.35 Investment analyst (capital projects)
034.40 Trust officer
034.45 Insurance broker
034.50 Underwriter (insurance)
034.98 Trainee
034.99 Other finance, investment and insurance specialist occupations

039 Company Secretarial, Accounting, Financial and Insurance Specialist Occupations (Excluding Clerical) Not Elsewhere Classified

039.10 Company registrar
039.20 Registrar of stocks and bonds
039.30 Committee secretary
039.40 Inspector of taxes
039.50 Tax consultant
039.98 Trainee
039.99 Other company secretarial, accounting, financial and insurance specialist occupations (excluding clerical) not elsewhere classified

04 Personnel and Management Services Specialist Occupations

041 Personnel Management and Industrial Relations Specialist Occupations

041.00 Manager
041.10 Personnel officer
041.20 Industrial relations officer
041.98 Trainee
041.99 Other personnel management and industrial relations specialist occupations

042 Operational Research, Organisation and Methods, Work Study and Related Specialist Occupations

042.05 Operational research officer
042.10 Organisation and methods officer
042.15 Work study officer
042.20 Methods engineer
042.25 Work measurement engineer
042.30 Management by objectives analyst
042.35 Standards engineer
042.40 Value analyst
042.45 Network analyst
042.50 Occupational analyst
042.98 Trainee
042.99 Other operational research, organisation and methods, work study and related specialist occupations

043 Economic, Statistical and Actuarial Specialist Occupations

043.10 Economist
043.20 Statistician
043.30 Actuary
043.98 Trainee
043.99 Other economic, statistical and actuarial specialist occupations

044 Automatic Data Processing (ADP) Planning and Programming Occupations

044.10 Data processing manager
044.20 Systems analyst
044.30 Computer programmer
044.98 Trainee
044.99 Other automatic data processing (ADP) planning and programming occupations

049 Personnel and Management Services Specialist Occupations Not Elsewhere Classified

049.10 Manager (management services)
049.98 Trainee
049.99 Other personnel and management service specialist occupations not elsewhere classified

05 Marketing, Advertising and Public Relations Specialist Occupations

051 Marketing, Advertising and Public Relations Specialist Occupations

051.05 Marketing manager
051.10 Market research analyst
051.15 Company sales manager
051.20 Advertising manager
051.25 Account executive (advertising agency)
051.30 Traffic and production executive (advertising)

051.35 Media planner
051.40 Advertisement manager
051.45 Public relations officer
051.98 Trainee
051.99 Marketing, advertising and public relations specialist occupations not elsewhere classified

06 Professional and Related Occupations Supporting Management and Administration Not Elsewhere Classified

061 Purchasing and Procurement Managers and Executives

061.00 Manager
061.10 Buyer (retail distribution)
061.20 Buyer (wholesale distribution)
061.30 Purchasing officer
061.40 Buyer (advertising space, time)
061.50 Print buyer (advertising)
061.60 Facilities procurement officer (television and film production)
061.98 Trainee
061.99 Other purchasing and procurement managers and executives

062 Property and Estate Management Occupations

062.10 Estate agent
062.20 Land agent
062.98 Trainee
062.99 Other property and estate management occupations

063 Library, Records, Information and Related Specialist Occupations

063.10 Librarian
063.20 Archivist
063.30 Information officer
063.40 Intelligence officer (Government service)
063.50 Curator (museum, art gallery or similar institution)

063.98 Trainee
063.99 Other library, records, information and related specialist occupations

064 Inspectors (Statutory and Similar Requirements)

064.05 Public health inspector
064.10 Pollution inspector (river authority or board)
064.15 Weights and measures inspector
064.20 Inspector of factories (HMFI)
064.25 Ship surveyor
064.30 Building inspector
064.35 Inspector (public utility installations)
064.40 Officer of customs and excise
064.45 Preventive officer (customs and excise, waterguard service)
064.50 Inspector (Royal Society for the Prevention of Cruelty to Animals)
064.55 Water bailiff (river authority or board)
064.60 Driving and traffic examiner
064.98 Trainee
064.99 Other inspectors (statutory and similar requirements)

069 Other Professional and Related Occupations Supporting Management and Administration

069.10 Personal assistant (management and administration)
069.20 National government officer (administrative or executive functions) (not elsewhere classified)
069.30 Local government officer (administrative or executive functions) (not elsewhere classified)
069.40 Appraiser (services standards)
069.98 Trainee
069.99 Other professional and related occupations supporting management and administration not elsewhere classified

Major Group III PROFESSIONAL AND RELATED OCCUPATIONS IN EDUCATION, WELFARE AND HEALTH

09 Teaching and Instructing Occupations

091 Teaching Occupations (University Education)

091.05 Vice-chancellor (university)
091.10 Teacher (education)
091.15 Teacher (health, medicine and dentistry)
091.20 Teacher (engineering)
091.25 Teacher (material, process and product technologies)
091.30 Teacher (agricultural, forestry and veterinary studies)
091.35 Teacher (science)
091.40 Teacher (social, administrative and business studies)

091.45 Teacher (English language and literature)
091.50 Teacher (foreign languages, literature and area studies)
091.55 Teacher (arts subjects excluding languages)
091.60 Teacher (music, drama and visual arts)
091.99 Other teaching occupations (university education)

092 Teaching Occupations (Teacher Training)

092.10 Principal (teacher training establishment)
092.20 Teacher

093 Teaching Occupations (Further Education) (Technical, Vocational and Related)

093 .10 Principal (further education establishment)
093 .20 Teacher (engineering and related studies)
093 .30 Teacher (material, process and product technologies)
093 .40 Teacher (science)
093 .50 Teacher (social studies)
093 .60 Teacher (administrative and business studies)
093 .70 Teacher (management service specialisations)
093 .99 Other teaching occupations (further education) (technical, vocational and related)

094 Teaching Occupations (Secondary Education)

094 .05 Headmaster (secondary education establishment)
094 .10 Teacher (science)
094 .15 Teacher (mathematics)
094 .20 Teacher (social studies)
094 .25 Teacher (commercial subjects)
094 .30 Teacher (domestic science)
094 .35 Teacher (technical subjects)
094 .40 Teacher (English language and literature)
094 .45 Teacher (foreign languages and literature)
094 .50 Teacher (arts subjects excluding languages)
094 .55 Teacher (music, drama and visual arts)
094 .99 Other teaching occupations (secondary education)

095 Teaching Occupations (Primary Education)

095 .10 Head teacher (primary school or department), Head teacher (preparatory school)
095 .20 Teacher (junior class), Teacher (preparatory school)
095 .30 Teacher (infant class)
095 .99 Other teaching occupations (primary education)

096 Teaching Occupations (Pre-Primary Education)

096 .10 Head teacher (pre-primary school)
096 .20 Teacher
096 .99 Other teaching occupations (pre-primary education)

097 Teaching Occupations (Special Education)

097 .10 Head teacher (school for physically, mentally handicapped children)
097 .20 Teacher (blind children)
097 .30 Teacher (deaf children)
097 .40 Teacher (mentally handicapped children)

097 .99 Other teaching occupations (special education)

098 Vocational Training Occupations

098 .10 Manager
098 .20 Vocational training instructor
098 .98 Trainee

099 Teaching and Instructing Occupations Not Elsewhere Classified

099 .00 Director of education
099 .01 Education officer
099 .05 Principal (educational or training establishment) not elsewhere classified
099 .10 Inspector of schools
099 .20 Inspector of training services
099 .30 Teacher (physical training)
099 .40 Teacher (diversionary activities)
099 .50 Private tutor
099 .60 Private music teacher
099 .70 Private dancing teacher
099 .80 Private driving instructor
099 .99 Other teaching and instructing occupations not elsewhere classified

10 Social Science, Welfare and Religious Occupations

101 Social Scientists and Related Occupations

101 .10 Sociologist
101 .20 Anthropologist
101 .30 Archaeologist
101 .40 Historian
101 .50 Philologist
101 .60 Psychologist
101 .70 Geographer
101 .99 Other social scientists and related occupations

102 Welfare Occupations

102 .00 Manager
102 .02 Social caseworker (general)
102 .04 Family caseworker
102 .06 Moral welfare worker
102 .08 Probation officer
102 .10 Inspector (National Society for the Prevention of Cruelty to Children)
102 .12 Visitor (National Society for the Prevention of Cruelty to Children)
102 .14 Child care officer
102 .16 Youth leader
102 .18 Matron (day, residential nursery)
102 .20 Residential child care worker (children's home)
102 .22 Residential child care worker (establishment for young offenders)
102 .24 Matron (old people's home)
102 .26 Welfare officer for the elderly
102 .28 Welfare officer for the physically handicapped
102 .30 Home teacher for the blind
102 .32 Welfare officer to the deaf
102 .34 Medical social worker
102 .36 Psychiatric social worker

102.38   Mental welfare officer
102.40   Leader (social group work)
102.42   Housing manager
102.44   Welfare officer (staff welfare)
102.46   Safety officer
102.98   Trainee
102.99   Other welfare occupations

103 Religious Occupations
103.10   Minister of religion
103.99   Other religious occupations

109 Social Science, Welfare and Religious Occupations Not Elsewhere Classified
109.10   Careers officer
109.20   Vocational guidance specialist
109.98   Trainee
109.99   Other social science, welfare and religious occupations not elsewhere classified

11 Health Diagnosing and Treating Occupations

111 Medical Practitioners
111.02   Medical administrator (national government)
111.04   Medical administrator (regional hospital board)
111.06   Medical administrator (hospital)
111.08   Medical officer of health
111.10   Consultant physician
111.15   Consultant surgeon
111.20   Consultant (gynaecology and obstetrics)
111.25   Anaesthetist
111.30   Psychiatrist
111.35   Radiologist
111.40   Registrar (hospital)
111.45   House officer (hospital)
111.50   Medical practitioner (general practice)
111.55   Industrial medical officer
111.60   Medical practitioner (public health)
111.65   Medical practitioner (teaching)
111.99   Other medical practitioners

112 Dental Practitioners
112.05   Dental administrator
112.10   Dental consultant
112.20   Dental practitioner (general practice)
112.30   Dental practitioner (teaching)
112.99   Other dental practitioners

113 Nursing Occupations
113.02   Nurse administrator (national government)
113.04   Nurse administrator (local government)
113.06   Nurse administrator (Council or Board for nurses or midwives)
113.08   Nursing officer (regional hospital board)
113.10   Nurse administrator (occupational health nursing)
113.20   Nurse administrator (hospital)
113.22   Charge nurse (ward)
113.24   Charge nurse (special department)
113.26   Midwifery sister
113.28   Charge nurse (theatre)
113.30   Staff nurse
113.32   Staff midwife
113.34   Hospital nurse (state enrolled nurse (SEN) and equivalent)
113.36   Nursing auxiliary, Nursing assistant
113.50   Domiciliary nurse
113.52   Private nurse
113.54   Domiciliary midwife
113.56   Health visitor
113.58   Clinic nurse
113.60   Surgery nurse
113.62   Occupational health nurse
113.64   School nurse
113.70   Nurse (teaching)
113.98   Trainee
113.99   Other nursing occupations

114 Pharmacists
114.10   Hospital pharmacist
114.20   Retail pharmacist
114.30   Industrial pharmacist
114.98   Trainee

115 Medical Radiographers
115.10   Diagnostic radiographer
115.20   Radiotherapeutic radiographer
115.98   Trainee
115.99   Other medical radiographers

116 Opticians
116.10   Opthalmic optician
116.20   Dispensing optician
116.98   Trainee

117 Physio-, Occupational, Speech and Related Therapists
117.10   Physiotherapist
117.20   Remedial gymnast
117.30   Osteopath
117.40   Masseur
117.50   Occupational therapist
117.60   Speech therapist
117.70   Orthoptist
117.98   Trainee
117.99   Other physio-, occupational, speech and related therapists

119 Health Diagnosing and Treating Occupations Not Elsewhere Classified
119.05   Dietitian
119.10   Chiropodist
119.15   Dental auxiliary
119.20   Dental hygienist
119.25   Cardiological technician
119.30   Electro-encephalography technician
119.35   Artificial limb fitter
119.40   Audiology technician
119.45   Pharmacy technician

119.98 Trainee
119.99 Other health diagnosing and treating occupations not elsewhere classified

12 Animal Health Occupations

121 Veterinarians
121.10 Veterinarian

129 Animal Health Occupations Not Elsewhere Classified
129.10 Animal health attendant
129.20 Laboratory technician (laboratory animal care)
129.98 Trainee
129.99 Other animal health occupations not elsewhere classified

Major Group IV LITERARY, ARTISTIC AND SPORTS OCCUPATIONS

15 Literary occupations

151 Editors, Writers, Journalists and Related Literary Occupations
151.05 Editor (newspaper, periodical)
151.10 Editor (books)
151.15 Editor (radio and television programmes)
151.20 Author
151.25 Critic
151.30 Reporter (press, radio, television), Writer (journalism)
151.35 Advertising copy writer
151.40 Publicity writer
151.45 Technical writer
151.50 Instruction writer (clerical and related procedures)
151.55 Process description writer (technical and scientific procedures)
151.60 Programme writer (programmed instruction)
151.98 Trainee
151.99 Other editors, writers, journalists and related literary occupations

159 Literary Occupations Not Elsewhere Classified
159.10 Translator, Interpreter
159.20 Monitor (radio broadcasts)
159.30 Literary agent
159.98 Trainee
159.99 Other literary occupations not elsewhere classified

16 Artists, Sculptors and Industrial Designers

161 Artists and Sculptors
161.10 Artist (excluding commercial and display)
161.20 Artist (commercial)
161.30 Sculptor
161.40 Etcher, Engraver
161.50 Interior decoration designer
161.60 Set designer (theatre, television), Art director (films)
161.70 Display artist
161.98 Trainee
161.99 Other artists and sculptors

162 Industrial Designers
162.00 Manager
162.05 Industrial designer (general)
162.10 Industrial designer (textiles, wallpapers, decorated plastics)
162.15 Industrial designer (furniture)
162.20 Industrial designer (clothing, fashion accessories)
162.25 Industrial designer (footwear)
162.30 Industrial designer (packaging)
162.35 Industrial designer (pottery)
162.40 Industrial designer (jewellery)
162.45 Industrial designer (motor vehicle bodywork and trim)
162.50 Industrial designer (engineering products)
162.55 Industrial designer (domestic appliances)
162.98 Trainee
162.99 Other industrial designers

17 Performing, Audio and Visual Arts Occupations Not Elsewhere Classified

171 Directors, Producers, Managers and Related Occupations (Performing, Audio and Visual Arts)
171.05 Producer (theatre, artistic production)
171.10 Producer (television, radio)
171.15 Director (films)
171.20 First assistant director (films)
171.25 Chief cameraman (films)
171.30 Lighting manager (television)
171.35 Stage manager (theatre)
171.40 Stage manager (television), Floor-manager (television)
171.45 Film editor
171.50 Assistant film editor
171.55 General manager (theatrical productions)
171.60 Touring manager (entertainment)
171.65 Producer (films)
171.70 Studio production manager (films)
171.75 Associate producer (films)
171.80 Unit production manager (films)
171.85 Casting director (films)
171.90 Programme operation assistant (radio)
171.98 Trainee

171.99 Other directors, producers, managers and related occupations (performing, audio and visual arts)

172 Musical Composers and Choreographers

172.10 Composer
172.20 Orchestrator, Arranger
172.30 Choreographer
172.99 Other musical composers and choreographers

173 Performers (Entertainment)

173.10 Conductor (musical)
173.20 Instrumentalist
173.30 Singer
173.40 Actor
173.50 Dancer
173.60 Acrobat
173.70 Comedian, Clown
173.80 Conjurer
173.90 Trainer (performing animals)
173.98 Trainee
173.99 Other performers (entertainment)

174 Photographers and Cameramen

174.10 Photographer (still camera)
174.20 Process camera operator (graphic reproduction)
174.30 Television cameraman
174.40 Film cameraman
174.50 Assistant film cameraman
174.60 Optical printer (cine film)
174.90 Photographer (snapshot)
174.98 Trainee
174.99 Other photographers and cameramen

175 Sound and Vision Equipment Operators (Artistic) (Excluding Cameramen)

175.05 Audio-visual aids operator
175.10 Projectionist
175.15 Telecine operator
175.20 Video tape recorder operator
175.25 Film recorder operator
175.30 Sound recordist
175.35 Sound mixer
175.40 Dubbing mixer
175.45 Microphone boom operator
175.98 Trainee
175.99 Other sound and vision equipment operators (artistic) (excluding cameramen)

179 Other Performing, Audio and Visual Arts Occupations

179.10 Announcer (radio, television)
179.20 Newsreader (radio, television)
179.30 Theatrical agent
179.40 Window dresser
179.50 Florist
179.60 Artist's model
179.70 Fashion model
179.98 Trainee
179.99 Other performing, audio and visual arts occupations not elsewhere classified

18 Professional Sportsmen, Coaches and Sports Officials

181 Professional Sportsmen, Coaches and Sports Officials

181.10 Team manager (sports and games)
181.20 Professional Association footballer
181.30 Jockey
181.40 Racing car driver, Racing motor cyclist
181.50 Professional sportsman (other)
181.60 Sports instructor, Coach
181.70 Sports official
181.98 Trainee

Major Group V PROFESSIONAL AND RELATED OCCUPATIONS IN SCIENCE, ENGINEERING, TECHNOLOGY AND SIMILAR FIELDS

21 Natural Sciences Research, Development, Technical Advisory, Consultancy and Related Occupations

211 Biological Scientists (Research, Development, Technical Advisory, Consultancy and Related Work)

211.00 Manager
211.05 Biologist
211.10 Zoologist
211.15 Botanist
211.20 Hydrobiologist
211.25 Parasitologist
211.30 Mycologist
211.35 Entomologist
211.40 Microbiologist
211.45 Taxonomist
211.50 Ecologist
211.55 Physiologist
211.60 Geneticist
211.65 Cytologist
211.70 Histologist
211.75 Pathologist
211.80 Pharmacologist
211.85 Agricultural scientist
211.98 Trainee
211.99 Other biological scientists (research, development, technical advisory, consultancy and related work)

212 Chemical Scientists (Research, Development, Analysis, Technical Advisory, Consultancy and Related Work)

212.00 Manager
212.11 General chemist (chemical or related products)

212.12 General chemist (food, drink, tobacco)
212.13 General chemist (glass, clay or related products)
212.14 General chemist (textiles)
212.15 General chemist (hides, skins, pelts, leather goods)
212.16 General chemist (paper, paper goods, printing)
212.17 General chemist (metals, alloys)
212.19 General chemist (other)
212.31 Chemist (research, development) (chemical or related products)
212.32 Chemist (research, development) (food, drink, tobacco)
212.33 Chemist (research, development) (glass, clay or related products)
212.34 Chemist (research, development) (textiles)
212.35 Chemist (research, development) (hides, skins, pelts, leather goods)
212.36 Chemist (research, development) (paper, paper goods, printing)
212.37 Chemist (research, development) (metals, alloys)
212.39 Chemist (research, development) (other)
212.51 Analytical chemist (chemical or related products)
212.52 Analytical chemist (food, drink, tobacco)
212.53 Analytical chemist (glass, clay or related products)
212.54 Analytical chemist (textiles)
212.55 Analytical chemist (hides, skins, pelts, leather goods)
212.56 Analytical chemist (paper, paper goods, printing)
212.57 Analytical chemist (metals, alloys)
212.59 Analytical chemist (other)
212.71 Chemist (consultancy and advice) (chemical or related products)
212.72 Chemist (consultancy and advice) (food, drink, tobacco)
212.73 Chemist (consultancy and advice) (glass, clay or related products)
212.74 Chemist (consultancy and advice) (textiles)
212.75 Chemist (consultancy and advice) (hides, skins, pelts, leather goods)
212.76 Chemist (consultancy and advice) (paper, paper goods, printing)
212.77 Chemist (consultancy and advice) (metals, alloys)
212.79 Chemist (consultancy and advice) (other)
212.98 Trainee
212.99 Other chemical scientists (research, development, analysis, technical advisory, consultancy and related work)

213 Physical Scientists (Research, Development, Technical Advisory, Consultancy and Related Work)

213.00 Manager
213.05 Physicist (general)
213.10 Physicist (heat)
213.15 Physicist (light)
213.20 Physicist (acoustics)
213.25 Physicist (mechanics)
213.30 Physicist (electricity and magnetism)
213.35 Physicist (electronics)
213.40 Physicist (solid state)
213.45 Physicist (nuclear)
213.50 Physicist (atomic and molecular)
213.55 Physicist (radiation protection)
213.60 Hospital physicist
213.65 Meteorologist
213.70 Astronomer
213.75 Geophysicist
213.98 Trainee
213.99 Other physical scientists (research, development, technical advisory, consultancy and related work)

214 Geological Scientists (Research, Development, Technical Advisory, Consultancy and Related Work)

214.00 Manager
214.10 Geologist
214.20 Mineralogist
214.30 Palaeontologist
214.98 Trainee
214.99 Other geological scientists (research, development, technical advisory, consultancy and related work)

215 Mathematicians

215.00 Manager
215.10 Mathematician (pure mathematics)
215.20 Mathematician (applied mathematics)
215.98 Trainee

219 Natural Sciences Research, Development, Technical Advisory, Consultancy and Related Occupations Not Elsewhere Classified

219.00 Manager
219.10 Biochemist
219.20 Biophysicist
219.30 Physical chemist
219.98 Trainee
219.99 Other natural sciences research, development, technical advisory, consultancy and related occupations not elsewhere classified

22 Engineering Research and Development, Design, Feasibility Studies, Applications, Liaison, Consultancy and Related Occupations

221 Civil and Structural Engineering Research and Development, Design, Feasibility Studies, Liaison, Consultancy and Related Occupations

221.00 Manager
221.11 General civil/structural engineer (general civil and structural engineering)

221 .12 General civil/structural engineer (building structures)

221 .13 General civil/structural engineer (harbour, dock, marine and related works)

221 .14 General civil/structural engineer (water supply, drainage, sewerage)

221 .15 General civil/structural engineer (roads and runways)

221 .16 General civil/structural engineer (bridges)

221 .17 General civil/structural engineer (tunnels)

221 .18 General civil/structural engineer (railway works)

221 .19 General civil/structural engineer (other civil and structural engineering)

221 .21 Civil/Structural engineer (research and development) (general civil and structural engineering)

221 .22 Civil/Structural engineer (research and development) (building structures)

221 .23 Civil/Structural engineer (research and development) (harbour, dock, marine and related works)

221 .24 Civil/Structural engineer (research and development) (water supply, drainage, sewerage)

221 .25 Civil/Structural engineer (research and development) (roads and runways)

221 .26 Civil/Structural engineer (research and development) (bridges)

221 .27 Civil/Structural engineer (research and development) (tunnels)

221 .28 Civil/Structural engineer (research and development) (railway works)

221 .29 Civil/Structural engineer (research and development) (other civil and structural engineering)

221 .31 Civil/Structural engineer (design) (general civil and structural engineering)

221 .32 Civil/Structural engineer (design) (building structures)

221 .33 Civil/Structural engineer (design) (harbour, dock, marine and related works)

221 .34 Civil/Structural engineer (design) (water supply, drainage, sewerage)

221 .35 Civil/Structural engineer (design) (roads and runways)

221 .36 Civil/Structural engineer (design) (bridges)

221 .37 Civil/Structural engineer (design) (tunnels)

221 .38 Civil/Structural engineer (design) (railway works)

221 .39 Civil/Structural engineer (design) (other civil and structural engineering)

221 .41 Civil/Structural engineer (feasibility studies) (general civil and structural engineering)

221 .42 Civil/Structural engineer (feasibility studies) (building structures)

221 .43 Civil/Structural engineer (feasibility studies) (harbour, dock, marine and related works)

221 .44 Civil/Structural engineer (feasibility studies) (water supply, drainage, sewerage)

221 .45 Civil/Structural engineer (feasibility studies) (roads and runways)

221 .46 Civil/Structural engineer (feasibility studies) (bridges)

221 .47 Civil/Structural engineer (feasibility studies) (tunnels)

221 .48 Civil/Structural engineer (feasibility studies) (railway works)

221 .49 Civil/Structural engineer (feasibility studies) (other civil and structural engineering)

221 .61 Civil/Structural engineer (liaison) (general civil and structural engineering)

221 .62 Civil/Structural engineer (liaison) (building structures)

221 .63 Civil/Structural engineer (liaison) (harbour, dock, marine and related works)

221 .64 Civil/Structural engineer (liaison) (water supply, drainage, sewerage)

221 .65 Civil/Structural engineer (liaison) (roads and runways)

221 .66 Civil/Structural engineer (liaison) (bridges)

221 .67 Civil/Structural engineer (liaison) (tunnels)

221 .68 Civil/Structural engineer (liaison) (railway works)

221 .69 Civil/Structural engineer (liaison) (other civil and structural engineering)

221 .71 Civil/Structural engineer (consultancy and advice) (general civil and structural engineering)

221 .72 Civil/Structural engineer (consultancy and advice) (building structures)

221 .73 Civil/Structural engineer (consultancy and advice) (harbour, dock, marine and related works)

221 .74 Civil/Structural engineer (consultancy and advice) (water supply, drainage, sewerage)

221 .75 Civil/Structural engineer (consultancy and advice) (roads and runways)

221 .76 Civil/Structural engineer (consultancy and advice) (bridges)

221 .77 Civil/Structural engineer (consultancy and advice) (tunnels)

221 .78 Civil/Structural engineer (consultancy and advice) (railway works)

221 .79 Civil/Structural engineer (consultancy and advice) (other civil and structural engineering)

221 .98 Trainee

221.99 Other civil and structural engineering research and development, design, feasibility studies, liaison, consultancy and related occupations

222 Mining, Quarrying and Drilling Engineers

222.00 Manager
222.10 Mining engineer (coal)
222.20 Mining engineer (ores and minerals other than coal)
222.30 Quarrying engineer
222.40 Natural gas engineer, Oil well engineer
222.98 Trainee
222.99 Other mining, quarrying and drilling engineers

223 Mechanical Engineering Research and Development, Design, Feasibility Studies, Applications, Liaison, Consultancy and Related Occupations

223.00 Manager
223.11 General mechanical engineer (general mechanical engineering)
223.12 General mechanical engineer (prime movers)
223.13 General mechanical engineer (mechanical instruments)
223.14 General mechanical engineer (aircraft and missile structures)
223.15 General mechanical engineer (vehicle chassis and bodies)
223.16 General mechanical engineer (ships' structures)
223.17 General mechanical engineer (mechanical plant, machinery and equipment)
223.19 General mechanical engineer (other mechanical engineering)
223.21 Mechanical engineer (research and development) (general mechanical engineering)
223.22 Mechanical engineer (research and development) (prime movers)
223.23 Mechanical engineer (research and development) (mechanical instruments)
223.24 Mechanical engineer (research and development) (aircraft and missile structures)
223.25 Mechanical engineer (research and development) (vehicle chassis and bodies)
223.26 Mechanical engineer (research and development) (ships' structures)
223.27 Mechanical engineer (research and development) (mechanical plant, machinery and equipment)
223.29 Mechanical engineer (research and development) (other mechanical engineering)
223.31 Mechanical engineer (design) (general mechanical engineering)
223.32 Mechanical engineer (design) (prime movers)
223.33 Mechanical engineer (design) (mechanical instruments)
223.34 Mechanical engineer (design) (aircraft and missile structures)
223.35 Mechanical engineer (design) (vehicle chassis and bodies)
223.36 Mechanical engineer (design) (ships' structures)
223.37 Mechanical engineer (design) (mechanical plant, machinery and equipment)
223.39 Mechanical engineer (design) (other mechanical engineering)
223.41 Mechanical engineer (feasibility studies) (general mechanical engineering)
223.42 Mechanical engineer (feasibility studies) (prime movers)
223.43 Mechanical engineer (feasibility studies) (mechanical instruments)
223.44 Mechanical engineer (feasibility studies) (aircraft and missile structures)
223.45 Mechanical engineer (feasibility studies) (vehicle chassis and bodies)
223.46 Mechanical engineer (feasibility studies) (ships' structures)
223.47 Mechanical engineer (feasibility studies) (mechanical plant, machinery and equipment)
223.49 Mechanical engineer (feasibility studies) (other mechanical engineering)
223.51 Mechanical engineer (applications) (general mechanical engineering)
223.52 Mechanical engineer (applications) (prime movers)
223.53 Mechanical engineer (applications) (mechanical instruments)
223.54 Mechanical engineer (applications) (aircraft and missile structures)
223.55 Mechanical engineer (applications) (vehicle chassis and bodies)
223.56 Mechanical engineer (applications) (ships' structures)
223.57 Mechanical engineer (applications) (mechanical plant, machinery and equipment)
223.59 Mechanical engineer (applications) (other mechanical engineering)
223.61 Mechanical engineer (liaison) (general mechanical engineering)
223.62 Mechanical engineer (liaison) (prime movers)
223.63 Mechanical engineer (liaison) (mechanical instruments)
223.64 Mechanical engineer (liaison) (aircraft and missile structures)
223.65 Mechanical engineer (liaison) (vehicle chassis and bodies)
223.66 Mechanical engineer (liaison) (ships' structures)
223.67 Mechanical engineer (liaison) (mechanical plant, machinery and equipment)
223.69 Mechanical engineer (liaison) (other mechanical engineering)

223.71 Mechanical engineer (consultancy and advice) (general mechanical engineering)
223.72 Mechanical engineer (consultancy and advice) (prime movers)
223.73 Mechanical engineer (consultancy and advice) (mechanical instruments)
223.74 Mechanical engineer (consultancy and advice) (aircraft and missile structures)
223.75 Mechanical engineer (consultancy and advice) (vehicle chassis and bodies)
223.76 Mechanical engineer (consultancy and advice) (ships' structures)
223.77 Mechanical engineer (consultancy and advice) (mechanical plant, machinery and equipment)
223.79 Mechanical engineer (consultancy and advice) (other mechanical engineering)
223.98 Trainee
223.99 Other mechanical engineering research and development, design, feasibility studies, applications, liaison, consultancy and related occupations

224 Electrical and Electronic Engineering Research and Development, Design, Feasibility Studies, Applications, Liaison, Consultancy and Related Occupations

224.00 Manager
224.11 General electrical/electronic engineer (general electrical and/or electronic engineering)
224.12 General electrical engineer (power generation, transmission and distribution systems)
224.13 General electrical/electronic engineer (telecommunication systems)
224.14 General electrical/electronic engineer (electronic data processing systems)
224.15 General electrical engineer (heavy electrical plant, equipment)
224.16 General electrical/electronic engineer (electrical and electronic instruments and appliances)
224.17 General electrical/electronic engineer (electrical and electronic components)
224.19 General electrical/electronic engineer (other electrical and/or electronic engineering)
224.21 Electrical/Electronic engineer (research and development) (general electrical and/or electronic engineering)
224.22 Electrical engineer (research and development) (power generation, transmission and distribution systems)

224.23 Electrical/Electronic engineer (research and development) (telecommunication systems)
224.24 Electrical/Electronic engineer (research and development) (electronic data processing systems)
224.25 Electrical engineer (research and development) (heavy electrical plant, equipment)
224.26 Electrical/Electronic engineer (research and development) (electrical and electronic instruments and appliances)
224.27 Electrical/Electronic engineer (research and development) (electrical and electronic components)
224.29 Electrical/Electronic engineer (research and development) (other electrical and/or electronic engineering)
224.31 Electrical/Electronic engineer (design) (general electrical and/or electronic engineering)
224.32 Electrical engineer (design) (power generation, transmission and distribution systems)
224.33 Electrical/Electronic engineer (design) (telecommunication systems)
224.34 Electrical/Electronic engineer (design) (electronic data processing systems)
224.35 Electrical engineer (design) (heavy electrical plant, equipment)
224.36 Electrical/Electronic engineer (design) (electrical and electronic instruments and appliances)
224.37 Electrical/Electronic engineer (design) (electrical and electronic components)
224.39 Electrical/Electronic engineer (design) (other electrical and/or electronic engineering)
224.41 Electrical/Electronic engineer (feasibility studies) (general electrical and/or electronic engineering)
224.42 Electrical engineer (feasibility studies) (power generation, transmission and distribution systems)
224.43 Electrical/Electronic engineer (feasibility studies) (telecommunication systems)
224.44 Electrical/Electronic engineer (feasibility studies) (electronic data processing systems)
224.45 Electrical engineer (feasibility studies) (heavy electrical plant, equipment)
224.46 Electrical/Electronic engineer (feasibility studies) (electrical and electronic instruments and appliances)
224.47 Electrical/Electronic engineer (feasibility studies) (electrical and electronic components)

224.49 Electrical/Electronic engineer (feasibility studies) (other electrical and/or electronic engineering)

224.51 Electrical/Electronic engineer (applications) (general electrical and/or electronic engineering)

224.52 Electrical engineer (applications) (power generation, transmission and distribution systems)

224.53 Electrical/Electronic engineer (applications) (telecommunication systems)

224.54 Electrical/Electronic engineer (applications) (electronic data processing systems)

224.55 Electrical engineer (applications) (heavy electrical plant, equipment)

224.56 Electrical/Electronic engineer (applications) (electrical and electronic instruments and appliances)

224.57 Electrical/Electronic engineer (applications) (electrical and electronic components)

224.59 Electrical/Electronic engineer (applications) (other electrical and/or electronic engineering)

224.61 Electrical/Electronic engineer (liaison) (general electrical and/or electronic engineering)

224.62 Electrical engineer (liaison) (power generation, transmission and distribution systems)

224.63 Electrical/Electronic engineer (liaison) (telecommunication systems)

224.64 Electrical/Electronic engineer (liaison) (electronic data processing systems)

224.65 Electrical engineer (liaison) (heavy electrical plant, equipment)

224.66 Electrical/Electronic engineer (liaison) (electrical and electronic instruments and appliances)

224.67 Electrical/Electronic engineer (liaison) (electrical and electronic components)

224.69 Electrical/Electronic engineer (liaison) (other electrical and/or electronic engineering)

224.71 Electrical/Electronic engineer (consultancy and advice) (general electrical and/or electronic engineering)

224.72 Electrical engineer (consultancy and advice) (power generation, transmission and distribution systems)

224.73 Electrical/Electronic engineer (consultancy and advice) (telecommunication systems)

224.74 Electrical/Electronic engineer (consultancy and advice) (electronic data processing systems)

224.75 Electrical engineer (consultancy and advice) (heavy electrical plant, equipment)

224.76 Electrical/Electronic engineer (consultancy and advice) (electrical and electronic instruments and appliances)

224.77 Electrical/Electronic engineer (consultancy and advice) (electrical and electronic components)

224.79 Electrical/Electronic engineer (consultancy and advice) (other electrical and/or electronic engineering)

224.98 Trainee

224.99 Other electrical and electronic engineering research and development, design, feasibility studies, applications, liaison, consultancy and related occupations

225 Chemical Engineering Research and Development, Design, Feasibility Studies, Applications, Liaison, Consultancy and Related Occupations

225.00 Manager

225.11 General chemical engineer (general chemical engineering)

225.12 General chemical engineer (heavy chemicals)

225.13 General chemical engineer (fine chemicals)

225.14 General chemical engineer (synthetic resins and plastics)

225.15 General chemical engineer (petroleum)

225.19 General chemical engineer (other chemical engineering)

225.21 Chemical engineer (research and development) (general chemical engineering)

225.22 Chemical engineer (research and development) (heavy chemicals)

225.23 Chemical engineer (research and development) (fine chemicals)

225.24 Chemical engineer (research and development) (synthetic resins and plastics)

225.25 Chemical engineer (research and development) (petroleum)

225.29 Chemical engineer (research and development) (other chemical engineering)

225.31 Chemical engineer (process and/or equipment design) (general chemical engineering)

225.32 Chemical engineer (process and/or equipment design) (heavy chemicals)

225.33 Chemical engineer (process and/or equipment design) (fine chemicals)

225.34 Chemical engineer (process and/or equipment design) (synthetic resins and plastics)

225.35 Chemical engineer (process and/or equipment design) (petroleum)

225.39 Chemical engineer (process and/or equipment design) (other chemical engineering)

225 .41 Chemical engineer (feasibility studies) (general chemical engineering)

225 .42 Chemical engineer (feasibility studies) (heavy chemicals)

225 .43 Chemical engineer (feasibility studies) (fine chemicals)

225 .44 Chemical engineer (feasibility studies) (synthetic resins and plastics)

225 .45 Chemical engineer (feasibility studies) (petroleum)

225 .49 Chemical engineer (feasibility studies) (other chemical engineering)

225 .51 Chemical engineer (applications) (general chemical engineering)

225 .52 Chemical engineer (applications) (heavy chemicals)

225 .53 Chemical engineer (applications) (fine chemicals)

225 .54 Chemical engineer (applications) (synthetic resins and plastics)

225 .55 Chemical engineer (applications) (petroleum)

225 .59 Chemical engineer (applications) (other chemical engineering)

225 .61 Chemical engineer (liaison) (general chemical engineering)

225 .62 Chemical engineer (liaison) (heavy chemicals)

225 .63 Chemical engineer (liaison) (fine chemicals)

225 .64 Chemical engineer (liaison) (synthetic resins and plastics)

225 .65 Chemical engineer (liaison) (petroleum)

225 .69 Chemical engineer (liaison) (other chemical engineering)

225 .71 Chemical engineer (consultancy and advice) (general chemical engineering)

225 .72 Chemical engineer (consultancy and advice) (heavy chemicals)

225 .73 Chemical engineer (consultancy and advice) (fine chemicals)

225 .74 Chemical engineer (consultancy and advice) (synthetic resins and plastics)

225 .75 Chemical engineer (consultancy and advice) (petroleum)

225 .79 Chemical engineer (consultancy and advice) (other chemical engineering)

225 .98 Trainee

225 .99 Other chemical engineering research and development, design, feasibility studies, applications, liaison, consultancy and related occupations

226 Production Engineers
226 .10 Production engineer
226 .98 Trainee

229 Engineering Research and Development, Design, Feasibility Studies, Applications, Liaison, Consultancy and Related Occupations Not Elsewhere Classified

229 .00 Manager
229 .10 Agricultural engineer
229 .20 Cathodic protection engineer
229 .30 Heating and ventilating engineer
229 .40 Instrumentation and control engineer
229 .50 Lubrication engineer
229 .60 Nuclear engineer
229 .70 Refrigeration engineer
229 .80 Traffic engineer
229 .90 General engineer
229 .98 Trainee
229 .99 Other engineering research and development, design, feasibility studies, applications, liaison, consultancy and related occupations not elsewhere classified

23 Technological (Excluding Engineering) Research and Development, Design, Feasibility Studies, Applications, Liaison, Consultancy and Related Occupations

231 Technological (Excluding Engineering) Research and Development, Design, Feasibility Studies, Applications, Liaison, Consultancy and Related Occupations

231 .00 Manager
231 .05 Metallurgist
231 .10 Glass technologist
231 .15 Ceramics technologist
231 .20 Rubber technologist
231 .25 Plastics technologist
231 .30 Textile technologist
231 .35 Fuel technologist
231 .40 Food technologist
231 .45 Brewer
231 .50 Packaging technologist
231 .98 Trainee
231 .99 Other technological (excluding engineering) research and development, design, feasibility studies, applications, liaison, consultancy and related occupations

24 Aircraft and Ships' Officers and Related Occupations

241 Flight Deck Officers
241 .05 Pilot-in-command (aeroplane over 12,500 lbs. total weight)
241 .10 Pilot-in-command (with crew) (aeroplane up to 12,500 lbs. total weight)
241 .15 Pilot-in-command (helicopter)
241 .20 Pilot-in-command (without crew) (aeroplane)

241.25 Co-pilot (aeroplane over 12,500 lbs. total weight)
241.30 Co-pilot (aeroplane up to 12,500 lbs. total weight)
241.35 Co-pilot (helicopter)
241.40 Test pilot (aircraft)
241.45 Flying instructor
241.50 Flight navigator
241.55 Flight engineer
241.98 Trainee
241.99 Other flight deck officers

242 Air Traffic Planning and Controlling Occupations
242.10 Flight planner
242.20 Flight operations officer
242.30 Area air traffic control officer
242.40 Air traffic control officer (local)
242.98 Trainee
242.99 Other air traffic planning and controlling occupations

243 Masters, Deck Officers and Pilots (Ship)
243.10 Master (foreign-going ship)
243.20 Master (home trade ship)
243.30 Skipper (river, harbour, dock, canal or other inland waterways craft)
243.40 Mate (foreign-going ship)
243.50 Mate (home trade ship)
243.60 Pilot (ship)
243.98 Trainee
243.99 Other masters, deck officers and pilots (ship)

244 Engineer and Radio Officers (Ship)
244.10 Chief engineer
244.20 Engineer officer
244.30 Radio officer
244.98 Trainee

249 Aircraft and Ships' Officers and Related Occupations Not Elsewhere Classified
249.10 Commander (hovercraft)
249.20 Engineer officer (hovercraft)
249.30 Navigator (hovercraft)
249.98 Trainee
249.99 Other aircraft and ships' officers and related occupations not elsewhere classified

25 Professional and Related Occupations in Science, Engineering, Technology and Similar Fields not Elsewhere Classified

251 Town Planners and Architects
251.10 Town planner
251.20 Architect (buildings)
251.30 Landscape architect
251.98 Trainee
251.99 Other town planners and architects

252 Surveyors
252.10 Land surveyor
252.20 Hydrographic surveyor, Marine surveyor
252.30 Mining surveyor
252.40 Building surveyor
252.50 Insurance surveyor
252.98 Trainee
252.99 Other surveyors

253 Draughtsmen
253.02 Chief draughtsman
253.04 Design draughtsman (general)
253.06 Design draughtsman (general mechanical engineering)
253.08 Design draughtsman (prime movers)
253.10 Design draughtsman (aircraft and missile structures)
253.12 Design draughtsman (vehicle chassis and bodies)
253.14 Design draughtsman (ship's structures)
253.16 Design draughtsman (mechanical plant, machinery and equipment)
253.18 Design draughtsman (electrical engineering)
253.20 Design draughtsman (electronic engineering)
253.22 Design draughtsman (heating, ventilating, refrigeration systems)
253.24 Draughtsman (instruments)
253.26 Draughtsman (plant layout)
253.28 Draughtsman (jig and tool)
253.30 Draughtman (civil, structural engineering)
253.32 Draughtsman (architectural)
253.34 Draughtsman (maps, charts, etc)
253.36 Detail draughtsman (general)
253.38 Detail draughtsman (mechanical engineering)
253.40 Detail draughtsman (ship's structures)
253.42 Detail draughtsman (electrical engineering)
253.44 Detail draughtsman (electronic engineering)
253.46 Detail draughtsman (heating, ventilating, refrigeration systems)
253.48 Detail draughtsman (pipework)
253.50 Drawing checker (technical drawings)
253.52 Map checker
253.54 Stressman
253.56 Technical illustrator
253.98 Trainee
253.99 Other draughtsmen

254 Laboratory Technicians and Similar Scientific Supporting Occupations
254.11 General laboratory technician (general science)
254.12 General laboratory technician (biology)
254.13 General laboratory technician (chemistry)
254.14 General laboratory technician (physics)

254.19 General laboratory technician (other science)

254.21 Medical laboratory technician

254.31 Laboratory technician (materials preparation) (general science)

254.32 Laboratory technician (materials preparation) (biology)

254.33 Laboratory technician (materials preparation) (chemistry)

254.34 Laboratory technician (materials preparation) (physics)

254.39 Laboratory technician (materials preparation) (other science)

254.41 Laboratory technician (analysis, measurement)

254.51 Laboratory technician (equipment operation)

254.98 Trainee

254.99 Other laboratory technicians and similar scientific supporting occupations

255 Architectural, Constructional and Related Technical Supporting Occupations Not Elsewhere Classified

255.10 Quantity surveyor

255.20 Technical assistant (quantity surveying)

255.30 Town planning assistant

255.40 Architectural technician

255.50 Civil engineering technician (general)

255.98 Trainee

255.99 Other architectural, constructional and related technical supporting occupations not elsewhere classified

256 Engineering (Excluding Architectural, Constructional and Related) Technical Supporting Occupations Not Elsewhere Classified

256.11 General technical assistant (mechanical engineering)

256.12 General technical assistant (electrical engineering)

256.13 General technical assistant (electronic engineering)

256.14 General technical assistant (chemical engineering)

256.19 General technical assistant (other engineering)

256.21 Technical controller (installation) (mechanical engineering)

256.22 Technical controller (installation) (electrical engineering)

256.23 Technical controller (installation) (electronic engineering)

256.24 Technical controller (installation (chemical engineering)

256.29 Technical controller (installation) (other engineering)

256.31 Test engineer (mechanical engineering)

256.32 Test engineer (electrical engineering)

256.33 Test engineer (electronic engineering)

256.34 Test engineer (chemical engineering)

256.39 Test engineer (other engineering)

256.41 Maintenance technician (mechanical engineering)

256.42 Maintenance technician (electrical engineering)

256.43 Maintenance technician (electronic engineering)

256.44 Maintenance technician (chemical engineering)

256.49 Maintenance technician (other engineering)

256.51 Technical service adviser (mechanical engineering)

256.52 Technical service adviser (electrical engineering)

256.53 Technical service adviser (electronic engineering)

256.54 Technical service adviser (chemical engineering)

256.59 Technical service adviser (other engineering)

256.98 Trainee

256.99 Other engineering (excluding architectural, constructional and related) technical supporting occupations not elsewhere classified

259 Other Professional and Related Occupations in Science, Engineering, Technology and Similar Fields

259.10 Planning engineer

259.20 Planner (numerical control)

259.30 Materials planner

259.40 Quality control engineer

259.50 Patent agent

259.60 Patent examiner

259.70 Technical assistant (technological)

259.98 Trainee

259.99 Other professional and related occupations in science, engineering, technology and similar fields not elsewhere classified

Major Group VI MANAGERIAL OCCUPATIONS (EXCLUDING GENERAL MANAGEMENT)

27 Managerial Occupations (Industrial Operations)

271 Managerial Occupations (Production Process) (Metal and Electrical)

271.11 Works manager (metal manufacture)

271.12 Works manager (general mechanical engineering products, prime movers, metal goods)

271.13 Works manager (aeronautical engineering products)

271.14 Works manager (automobile engineering, vehicle building)

271.15 Shipyard manager

271.16 Works manager (electrical engineering products)

271.17 Works manager (electronic engineering products)

271.19 Works manager (metal and electrical) (other)

271.31 Production control manager (metal manufacture)

271.32 Production control manager (general mechanical engineering products, prime movers, metal goods)

271.33 Production control manager (aeronautical engineering products)

271.34 Production control manager (automobile engineering, vehicle building)

271.35 Production control manager (shipbuilding)

271.36 Production control manager (electrical engineering products)

271.37 Production control manager (electronic engineering products)

271.39 Production control manager (metal and electrical) (other)

271.51 Production superintendent (metal manufacture)

271.52 Production superintendent (general mechanical engineering products, prime movers, metal goods)

271.53 Production superintendent (aeronautical engineering products)

271.54 Production superintendent (automobile engineering, vehicle building)

271.55 Production superintendent (shipbuilding)

271.56 Production superintendent (electrical engineering products)

271.57 Production superintendent (electronic engineering products)

271.59 Production superintendent (metal and electrical) (other)

271.71 Production executive (metal manufacture)

271.72 Production executive (general mechanical engineering products, prime movers, metal goods)

271.73 Production executive (aeronautical engineering products)

271.74 Production executive (automobile engineering, vehicle building)

271.75 Production executive (shipbuilding)

271.76 Production executive (electrical engineering products)

271.77 Production executive (electronic engineering products)

271.79 Production executive (metal and electrical) (other)

271.98 Trainee

271.99 Other managerial occupations (production process) (metal and electrical)

272 Managerial Occupations (Production Process) (Excluding Metal and Electrical)

272.11 Works manager (hides, skins, pelts, leather goods)

272.12 Works manager (textiles, clothing)

272.13 Works manager (chemical, coal, petroleum or related products)

272.14 Works manager (food, drink, tobacco)

272.15 Works manager (paper, paper goods, printing)

272.16 Works manager (glass, clay or related products)

272.17 Works manager (woodworking, upholstery or related products)

272.19 Works manager (other)

272.31 Production control manager (hides, skins, pelts, leather goods)

272.32 Production control manager (textiles, clothing)

272.33 Production control manager (chemical, coal, petroleum or related products)

272.34 Production control manager (food, drink, tobacco)

272.35 Production control manager (paper, paper goods, printing)

272.36 Production control manager (glass, clay or related products)

272.37 Production control manager (woodworking, upholstery or related products)

272.39 Production control manager (other)

272.51 Production superintendent (hides, skins, pelts, leather goods)

272.52 Production superintendent (textiles, clothing)

272.53 Production superintendent (chemical, coal, petroleum or related products)

272.54 Production superintendent (food, drink, tobacco)

272.55 Production superintendent (paper, paper goods, printing)

272.56 Production superintendent (glass, clay or related products)
272.57 Production superintendent (woodworking, upholstery or related products)
272.59 Production superintendent (other)
272.71 Production executive (hides, skins, pelts, leather goods)
272.72 Production executive (textiles, clothing)
272.73 Production executive (chemical, coal, petroleum or related products)
272.74 Production executive (food, drink, tobacco)
272.75 Production executive (paper, paper goods, printing)
272.76 Production executive (glass, clay or related products)
272.77 Production executive (woodworking, upholstery or related products)
272.79 Production executive (other)
272.98 Trainee
272.99 Other managerial occupations (production process) (excluding metal and electrical)

273 Managerial Occupations (Engineering Maintenance)

273.10 Maintenance manager (plant, machinery, equipment)
273.20 Maintenance manager (motor vehicles)
273.30 Motive power superintendent (railways)
273.40 Maintenance manager (aircraft)
273.98 Trainee
273.99 Other managerial occupations (engineering maintenance)

274 Managerial Occupations (Construction)

274.05 Contracts manager
274.10 Site agent
274.15 Sub-agent
274.20 Site engineer
274.25 General foreman (construction)
274.30 Resident engineer
274.35 Clerk of works
274.40 Manager (small works)
274.45 Maintenance manager (buildings and other structures)
274.98 Trainee
274.99 Other managerial occupations (building and civil engineering)

275 Managerial Occupations (Mining, Quarrying and Well Drilling)

275.10 Mine manager
275.20 Under-manager (mining)
275.30 Overman (mining)
275.40 Quarry manager
275.50 Manager (well drilling operations)
275.98 Trainee
275.99 Other managerial occupations (mining, quarrying and well drilling)

276 Managerial Occupations (Production and Supply of Gas, Water and Electricity)

276.10 Manager (gas production, supply)
276.20 Manager (water supply)
276.30 Manager (electricity production, transmission)
276.40 Manager (utilities)
276.98 Trainee
276.99 Other managerial occupations (production and supply of gas, water and electricity)

277 Managerial Occupations (Transport Operating, Warehousing and Materials Handling)

277.02 Traffic manager (transport undertaking)
277.04 Traffic manager (company)
277.06 Operating manager (transport undertaking)
277.08 Transport fleet manager (company transport)
277.10 Schedules planning manager (transport)
277.12 Harbour master
277.14 Dock master
277.16 Pier master
277.18 Berthing superintendent
277.20 Marine superintendent
277.22 Ships' agent
277.24 Airport manager
277.26 Station manager (airline)
277.28 Station manager (railway)
277.30 Manager (bus, coach station)
277.32 Distribution manager
277.34 Stock control manager
277.36 Stores manager
277.38 Warehouse manager
277.40 Manager (loading, unloading and related operations)
277.98 Trainee
277.99 Other managerial occupations (transport operating, warehousing and materials handling)

279 Managerial Occupations (Industrial Operations) Not Elsewhere Classified

279.10 Manager (laundering, dyeing, dry cleaning operations)
279.98 Trainee
279.99 Other managerial occupations (industrial operations) not elsewhere classified

28 Managerial Occupations (Services and Not Elsewhere Classified)

281 Managerial Occupations (Office)

281.02 Office manager (general)
281.04 Office manager (accounts)
281.06 Office manager (credit control)
281.08 Office manager (sales office)
281.10 Office manager (freight shipment and transportation)
281.12 Office manager (records)

281.14 Office manager (statistics)
281.16 Office manager (insurance)
281.18 Computer operations manager
281.20 Office manager (travel bookings)
281.22 Branch manager (bank)
281.24 Branch manager (building society)
281.26 Branch manager (private employment agency)
281.28 Manager (employment exchange)
281.30 Manager (social security office)
281.32 Office manager (tax office)
281.34 Registrar (births, deaths, marriages)
281.36 Manager (post office)
281.38 Manager (radio, telegraph, teleprinter installation)
281.40 Area telephone manager
281.42 Telephone exchange superintendent
281.98 Trainee
281.99 Other managerial occupations (office)

282 Managerial Occupations (Wholesale Distributive Trade)

282.10 Manager (wholesale distribution) (excluding cash and carry)
282.20 Manager (cash and carry wholesale)
282.98 Trainee
282.99 Other managerial occupations (wholesale distributive trade)

283 Managerial Occupations (Retail Distributive Trade)

283.10 Manager (departmental store or similar establishment)
283.20 Manager (supermarket or similar establishment)
283.30 Manager (branch retail shop excluding departmental store, supermarket or similar)
283.40 Manager (independent retail shop excluding departmental store, supermarket or similar)
283.50 Departmental manager (shop, store, supermarket)
283.60 Shopkeeper
283.98 Trainee
283.99 Other managerial occupations (retail distributive trade)

284 Managerial Occupations (Catering, Hotels and Public Houses)

284.05 Manager (hotel, guest house, residential club) (licensed)
284.10 Manager (hotel, guest house, residential club) (unlicensed)
284.15 Purser
284.20 Warden (hostel, lodging house)
284.25 Head housekeeper
284.30 Catering manager (hotel)
284.35 Catering manager (institution)
284.40 Catering manager (industrial catering)
284.45 Manager (public restaurant, club restaurant) (table service)
284.50 Banqueting manager
284.55 Manager (public restaurant, club restaurant) (cafeteria service)
284.60 Canteen manager
284.65 Manager (snack bar)
284.70 Publican
284.75 Innkeeper
284.80 Club steward
284.98 Trainee
284.99 Other managerial occupations (catering, hotels and public houses)

285 Managerial Occupations (Recreation and Amenity Services)

285.05 Manager (general recreational facilities)
285.10 Manager (cultural facilities)
285.15 Entertainment manager
285.20 Manager (sports centre)
285.25 Stadium manager
285.30 Baths manager
285.35 Manager (theatre, concert hall)
285.40 Cinema manager
285.45 Manager (bowling alley)
285.50 Manager (bingo hall)
285.98 Trainee
285.99 Other managerial occupations (recreation and amenity services)

286 Managerial Occupations (Farming, Fishing and Related)

286.05 Manager (arable and livestock farm)
286.10 Manager (arable farm)
286.15 Manager (mixed livestock farm)
286.20 Manager (cattle, dairy farm)
286.25 Manager (sheep farm)
286.30 Manager (pig farm)
286.35 Manager (poultry farm)
286.40 Manager (animal-keeping establishment excluding livestock farm)
286.45 Manager (horticultural undertaking)
286.50 Forest officer
286.55 Skipper (fishing vessel)
286.60 Manager (oyster, mussel or clam cultivation)
286.98 Trainee
286.99 Other managerial occupations (farming, fishing and related)

287 Officers (Armed Forces) Not Elsewhere Classified

287.10 Officer (armed forces) not elsewhere classified
287.98 Cadet (armed forces) not elsewhere classified

288 Managerial Occupations (Police, Fire Fighting and Related Protective Services)

288.10 Senior officer (police force)
288.20 Senior officer (fire brigade)
288.30 Senior officer (salvage corps)
288.40 Governor (prison or similar institution)
288.50 Manager (security)
288.98 Trainee
288.99 Other managerial occupations (police, fire fighting and related protective services)

289 Managerial Occupations (Administration and Not Elsewhere Classified)

289.00 Manager (unspecified)
289.05 Administration manager
289.10 Registrar (educational establishment)
289.15 Manager (common services)
289.20 Manager (services development)
289.25 Manager (hire of plant, equipment, machinery or related items)
289.30 Manager (small equipment servicing)
289.35 Manager (cleaning and related services)
289.40 Manager (hairdressing, beauty treatment)
289.45 Ambulance station superintendent
289.50 Cemetery superintendent
289.55 Manager (cleansing, refuse disposal)
289.60 Sewage works manager
289.98 Trainee
289.99 Other managerial occupations (administration and not elsewhere classified)

Major Group VII CLERICAL AND RELATED OCCUPATIONS

31 Clerical Occupations

310 Supervisors (Clerical Occupations)

310.10 Supervisor (costing and accounting clerical occupations)
310.20 Supervisor (cash handling clerical occupations)
310.30 Supervisor (finance and investment clerical occupations)
310.40 Supervisor (insurance clerical occupations)
310.50 Supervisor (production and materials controlling clerical occupations)
310.60 Supervisor (shipment and travel arranging clerical occupations)
310.70 Supervisor (record keeping and library clerical occupations)
310.80 Supervisor (general clerical occupations)
310.98 Trainee
310.99 Other supervisors (clerical occupations)

311 Costing and Accounting Clerical Occupations

311.05 Audit clerk
311.10 Book-keeper
311.15 Cost clerk
311.20 Stocktaker
311.25 Wages clerk
311.50 Invoice clerk
311.55 Ledger clerk
311.98 Trainee
311.99 Other costing and accounting clerical occupations

312 Cash Handling Clerical Occupations

312.05 Bank cashier
312.10 Counter cashier (building society office)
312.15 Post office counter clerk
312.20 Office cashier (not elsewhere classified)
312.50 Cash collector
312.55 Ticket-issuing clerk
312.60 Counter clerk (betting)
312.65 Casino cashier
312.90 Cash desk clerk
312.91 Check-out operator
312.92 Pay-out clerk
312.93 Coin collector (meters)
312.94 Fee collector (toll, parking)
312.98 Trainee
312.99 Other cash handling clerical occupations

313 Finance, Investment and Insurance Clerical Occupations

313.05 Foreign exchange clerk (banking)
313.10 Securities clerk
313.15 Stockbroker's clerk
313.20 Clerk (share and stock registration)
313.25 Insurance clerk (insurance company)
313.30 Insurance broker's clerk
313.35 Insurance clerk (excluding insurance broker's or insurance company)
313.40 Average adjuster's clerk
313.45 Probate clerk
313.98 Trainee
313.99 Other finance, investment and insurance clerical occupations

314 Production and Materials Controlling Clerical Occupations

314.05 Planning clerk
314.10 Purchasing clerk
314.15 Stock control clerk
314.20 Dispatch clerk, Sales order clerk
314.25 Telephone sales order clerk (services)
314.50 Progress clerk
314.55 Schedule clerk
314.60 Checker (goods, raw materials)
314.65 Milk recorder
314.98 Trainee
314.99 Other production and materials controlling clerical occupations

315 Shipment and Travel Arranging Clerical Occupations

315.05 Freight clerk (export, import)
315.10 Freight clerk (inland transport)
315.15 Load control clerk (air transport)
315.20 Chartering clerk (sea transport)
315.25 Schedules clerk (transport services)
315.30 Traffic dispatcher (air transport)

315.35 Reservations clerk (travel)
315.50 Travel enquiry clerk
315.98 Trainee
315.99 Other shipment and travel arranging clerical occupations

316 Record Keeping and Library Clerical Occupations

316.10 Library assistant
316.20 Library clerk (automatic data records)
316.30 Press cuttings clerk
316.50 Time clerk
316.60 Records clerk (not elsewhere classified)
316.90 Filing clerk
316.98 Trainee
316.99 Other record keeping and library clerical occupations

319 General Clerical Occupations and Clerical Occupations Not Elsewhere Classified

319.02 General clerk
319.04 Correspondence clerk
319.06 Statistical clerk
319.08 Control clerk (data processing)
319.10 Conveyancing clerk
319.12 Litigation clerk
319.14 Justices' clerk's assistant
319.16 Clerk (advertising, publicity)
319.18 Employment clerk
319.20 Calculator, Declarator
319.22 Design copyist (roller engraving, block cutting)
319.24 Design transferrer (printing rollers, blocks)
319.26 Design copyist (weaving, knitting, lace making, etc)
319.28 Tracer (drawing office)
319.30 Continuity clerk (film making)
319.32 Reader (printing)
319.50 Routine clerk (multiple tasks) (not elsewhere classified)
319.52 Information clerk
319.54 Research survey clerk
319.56 Hotel receptionist
319.58 Receptionist (health diagnosing and treating services)
319.60 Receptionist (not elsewhere classified)
319.90 Routine clerk (single task) (not elsewhere classified)
319.92 Copyholder (printing)
319.98 Trainee
319.99 Other general clerical occupations and clerical occupations not elsewhere classified

32 Shorthand, Typewriting and Related Secretarial Occupations

320 Supervisors (Shorthand, Typewriting and Related Secretarial Occupations)

320.10 Supervisor (shorthand, typewriting and related secretarial occupations)
320.98 Trainee

321 Shorthand Writing and Related Occupations

321.10 Secretary shorthand typist
321.20 Shorthand typist
321.30 Shorthand typist (foreign language)
321.40 Shorthand writer
321.98 Trainee
321.99 Other shorthand writing and related occupations

322 Typewriting Occupations

322.10 Secretary typist
322.50 Audio typist
322.60 Copy typist
322.98 Trainee
322.99 Other typewriting occupations

33 Office Machine Operating Occupations (Excluding Telecommunications)

330 Supervisors (Office Machine Operating Occupations (Excluding Telecommunications))

330.10 Supervisor (accounting and calculating machine operators)
330.20 Supervisor (automatic data processing equipment operating occupations)
330.30 Supervisor (key-punch operating occupations)
330.98 Trainee
330.99 Other supervisors (office machine operating occupations (excluding telecommunications))

331 Accounting and Calculating Machine Operators

331.10 Accounting machine operator
331.50 Calculating machine operator
331.98 Trainee

332 Automatic Data Processing Equipment Operating Occupations

332.10 Computer operator
332.50 Data processing equipment operator (excluding computer)
332.90 Sorting machine operator (punched cards)
332.98 Trainee
332.99 Other automatic data processing equipment operating occupations

333 Key-punch Operating Occupations

333.10 Key-punch operator (alphanumeric keyboard)
333.20 Verifier operator
333.50 Key-punch operator (numeric keyboard)
333.98 Trainee
333.99 Other key-punch operating occupations

334 Document Reproducing Machine Operating Occupations

334 .10 Photocopying machine operator
334 .20 Duplicating machine operator (excluding offset)
334 .98 Trainee
334 .99 Other document reproducing machine operating occupations

339 Office Machine Operating Occupations (Excluding Telecommunications) Not Elsewhere Classified

339 .10 Addressing machine operator
339 .98 Trainee
339 .99 Other office machine operating occupations (excluding telecommunications) not elsewhere classified

34 Telecommunications Operating and Mail Distributing Occupations

340 Supervisors (Telecommunications Operating and Mail Distributing Occupations)

340 .10 Supervisor (telephone operators)
340 .20 Supervisor (radio operating occupations)
340 .30 Supervisor (telegraphic equipment operating occupations)
340 .40 Supervisor (mail, parcel and message distributing occupations)

340 .98 Trainee
340 .99 Other supervisors (telecommunications operating and mail distributing occupations)

341 Telephone Operators

341 .10 Telephone operator (public telephone exchange)
341 .20 Telephone operator (private branch exchange)
341 .98 Trainee

342 Radio and Telegraphic Equipment Operating Occupations

342 .10 Radio operator
342 .20 Teleprinter operator
342 .30 Radio telephone operator
342 .40 Air traffic control assistant
342 .50 Port control signalman
342 .98 Trainee
342 .99 Other radio and telegraphic equipment operating occupations

343 Mail, Parcel and Message Distributing Occupations

343 .10 Sorter (mail)
343 .50 Postman
343 .90 Messenger
343 .98 Trainee
343 .99 Other mail, parcel and message distributing occupations

Major Group VIII SELLING OCCUPATIONS

36 Selling Occupations (Distributive Trade)

360 Supervisors (Selling Occupations (Distributive Trade))

360 .10 Sales supervisor
360 .20 Supervisor (roundsmen)
360 .98 Trainee
360 .99 Other supervisors (selling occupations (distributive trade))

361 Salesmen and Shop Assistants

361 .02 Shop assistant (general)
361 .04 Salesman (motor vehicles, motor cycles)
361 .06 Salesman (machinery and related equipment)
361 .08 Shop assistant (antiques and objets d'art)
361 .10 Shop assistant (books)
361 .12 Shop assistant (boots and shoes)
361 .14 Shop assistant (building materials, tools)
361 .16 Shop assistant (clothing)
361 .18 Shop assistant (corn and seed merchants, pet stores)
361 .20 Shop assistant (cosmetics, toiletries, perfumeries)

361 .22 Shop assistant (cycles, games, toys, sports equipment, leather and travel goods, baby carriages)
361 .24 Shop assistant (domestic hardware, china, glass)
361 .26 Shop assistant (electrical, electronic equipment)
361 .28 Shop assistant (engineering components, motor accessories)
361 .30 Shop assistant (flowers, plants)
361 .32 Shop assistant (furniture, floor coverings)
361 .34 Shop assistant (jewellery, watches, clocks)
361 .36 Shop assistant (musical instruments, sheet music, records, tapes)
361 .38 Shop assistant (newspapers, stationery, confectionery, tobacco)
361 .40 Shop assistant (pharmaceutical goods)
361 .42 Shop assistant (photographic equipment, optical or scientific instruments)
361 .44 Shop assistant (soft furnishings and fabrics, household linen, haberdashery, wool, art needlework)
361 .46 Shop assistant (bread, cakes, flour confectionery)

361 .48 Shop assistant (fish, poultry, game)
361 .50 Shop assistant (greengroceries)
361 .52 Shop assistant (groceries, provisions)
361 .54 Shop assistant (meat, delicatessen)
361 .56 Shop assistant (wines, spirits)
361 .58 Receiving office assistant
361 .90 Shop assistant (sundries)
361 .92 Petrol service station attendant
361 .98 Trainee
361 .99 Other salesmen and shop assistants

362 Roundsmen

362 .10 Roundsman (food and drink)
362 .20 Roundsman (goods excluding food and drink)
362 .30 Roundsman (laundry and similar services)
362 .98 Trainee
362 .99 Other roundsmen

363 Street Trading Occupations

363 .10 Driver-salesman (mobile shop, van)
363 .20 Stall salesman
363 .99 Other street trading occupations

369 Selling Occupations (Distributive Trade) Not Elsewhere Classified

369 .10 Demonstrator
369 .98 Trainee
369 .99 Other selling occupations (distributive trade) not elsewhere classified

37 Sales Representatives, Agents and Related Occupations

371 Technical Sales Representatives

371 .05 Technical sales representative (industrial plant, machinery and equipment, excluding instruments)
371 .10 Technical sales representative (mechanical engineering components)
371 .15 Technical sales representative (instruments)
371 .20 Technical sales representative (electrical and electronic equipment, excluding instruments)
371 .25 Technical sales representative (electrical and electronic engineering components)
371 .30 Technical sales representative (heating, ventilating, air-conditioning and refrigeration systems)
371 .35 Technical sales representative (industrial materials)
371 .40 Technical sales representative (agricultural supplies)
371 .45 Technical sales representative (medical supplies)

371 .98 Trainee
371 .99 Other technical sales representatives

372 Sales Representatives (Wholesale Goods)

372 .05 Field sales superintendent (wholesale goods)
372 .10 Sales representative (food, non-alcoholic drinks)
372 .15 Sales representative (alcoholic drinks)
372 .20 Sales representative (tobacco products)
372 .25 Sales representative (clothing, footwear)
372 .30 Sales representative (household requirements, domestic appliances)
372 .35 Sales representative (toiletries, fancy goods)
372 .40 Sales representative (office equipment and supplies)
372 .98 Trainee
372 .99 Other sales representatives (wholesale goods)

373 Sales Representatives (Property and Services)

373 .10 Property negotiator (estate agency)
373 .20 Auctioneer
373 .30 Insurance inspector
373 .40 Insurance agent
373 .50 Sales representative (office, commercial and similar services)
373 .60 Sales representative (cleaning, security and similar services)
373 .98 Trainee
373 .99 Other sales representatives (property and services)

379 Sales Representatives, Agents and Related Occupations Not Elsewhere Classified

379 .10 Commodity broker
379 .20 Importer
379 .30 Exporter
379 .40 Shipbroker
379 .50 Airbroker
379 .90 Door-to-door canvasser (goods)
379 .95 Door-to-door canvasser (household services)
379 .98 Trainee
379 .99 Other sales representatives, agents and related occupations not elsewhere classified

Major Group IX SECURITY AND PROTECTIVE SERVICE OCCUPATIONS

40 Armed Forces Occupations Not Elsewhere Classified

400 Warrant Officers, Petty Officers and Other Non-commissioned Officers Not Elsewhere Classified
- 400.10 Non-commissioned officer

401 Other Ranks (Armed Forces) Not Elsewhere Classified
- 401.10 Member of armed forces
- 401.98 Trainee

41 Police, Fire Fighting and Related Protective Service Occupations

410 Sergeants and Other Supervisors (Police, Fire Fighting and Related Protective Service Occupations)
- 410.10 Police sergeant (civil police)
- 410.20 Police sergeant (excluding civil police)
- 410.30 Supervisor (fire fighting, fire prevention and salvage workers)
- 410.40 Principal officer (prison service)
- 410.50 Chief security officer (private undertaking)
- 410.99 Other sergeants and supervisors (police, fire fighting and related protective service occupations)

411 Policemen (Statutory Forces)
- 411.10 Police constable (civil police)
- 411.20 Police constable (excluding civil police)
- 411.98 Trainee
- 411.99 Other policemen (statutory forces)

412 Fire Fighting, Fire Prevention and Salvage Occupations
- 412.10 Fireman (public fire service)
- 412.20 Fireman (private fire service)
- 412.30 Fire prevention officer
- 412.40 Fire point inspection man
- 412.50 Salvage man
- 412.98 Trainee
- 412.99 Other fire fighting, fire prevention and salvage occupations

419 Police, Fire Fighting and Related Protective Service Occupations Not Elsewhere Classified
- 419.10 Coastguard
- 419.20 Prison officer
- 419.30 County court bailiff (England and Wales), Sheriff officer (Scotland)
- 419.50 Store detective
- 419.55 Hotel detective
- 419.60 Private detective
- 419.65 Security officer (private undertaking)
- 419.70 Patrolman (security organisation)
- 419.75 Security guard
- 419.90 Gate-keeper
- 419.91 Park keeper
- 419.92 Estate ranger
- 419.93 Traffic warden
- 419.98 Trainee
- 419.99 Other police, fire fighting and related protective service occupations not elsewhere classified

Major Group X CATERING, CLEANING, HAIRDRESSING AND OTHER PERSONAL SERVICE OCCUPATIONS

43 Food and Beverage Preparing, Serving and Related Occupations

430 Supervisors (Food and Beverage Preparing, Serving and Related Occupations)
- 430.10 Chef de cuisine (hotel, club, restaurant), Sous chef (hotel, club, restaurant)
- 430.20 Head chef (industrial, institutional catering), Head cook (industrial, institutional catering)
- 430.30 Chef de partie
- 430.40 Head waiter (silver service)
- 430.50 Head waiter (plate service)
- 430.60 Head barman
- 430.70 Supervisor (food and beverage dispensers and counter hands)
- 430.98 Trainee
- 430.99 Other supervisors (food and beverage preparing, serving and related occupations)

431 Cooks (Catering Services)
- 431.05 Chef (gourmet fare)
- 431.10 Chef (plain fare)
- 431.15 Cook (foreign fare)
- 431.20 Cook (private household)
- 431.25 Cook (ship's galley)
- 431.30 Pastry cook (plain fare)
- 431.50 Fish fryer
- 431.90 Assistant cook
- 431.98 Trainee
- 431.99 Other cooks

432 Waiters and Waitresses
- 432.10 Waiter (silver service)
- 432.20 Wine waiter

432.50 Waiter (plate service)
432.98 Trainee
432.99 Other waiters and waitresses

433 Barmen, Barmaids and Bar Stewards

433.10 Barman (general)
433.20 Barman (cocktail bar)
433.30 Barman (dispense bar)
433.50 Bar waiter
433.98 Trainee
433.99 Other barmen, barmaids and bar stewards

434 Food and Beverage Dispensers and Counter Hands (Catering Services)

434.10 Food and beverages dispenser (table service)
434.20 Counter assistant (public cafeteria, buffet, snack bar)
434.30 Counter assistant (industrial restaurant)
434.98 Trainee
434.99 Other food and beverage dispensers and counter hands (catering services)

435 Kitchen and Dining-Room Hands

435.10 Kitchen assistant
435.20 Washer-up
435.30 Kitchen porter
435.40 Table clearer (catering)
435.98 Trainee
435.99 Other kitchen and dining-room hands

439 Food and Beverage Preparing, Serving and Related Occupations Not Elsewhere Classified

439.10 Carver
439.98 Trainee
439.99 Other food and beverage preparing, serving and related occupations not elsewhere classified

44 Housekeepers, Personal Service Attendants and Related Occupations (Excluding Cleaners)

440 Supervisors (Housekeepers, Personal Service Attendants and Related Occupations (Excluding Cleaners))

440.10 Housekeeper (supervising)
440.20 Butler
440.30 Chief steward (seagoing), Second steward (seagoing)
440.40 Chief air steward
440.50 Supervisor (ward orderlies and medical attendants)
440.98 Trainee
440.99 Other supervisors (porters and attendants and housekeepers and related personal service occupations)

441 Housekeepers, Maids and Related Personal Service Occupations

441.05 Working housekeeper (private household)
441.10 Companion

441.15 Valet
441.20 Lady's maid
441.25 Nursery nurse
441.30 Nursery assistant
441.35 Wardrobe mistress
441.50 Dresser (theatrical)
441.55 Batman
441.60 Nanny
441.65 School helper
441.70 Schoolchildren's supervisor
441.75 General maid (private household)
441.80 General maid (excluding private household)
441.85 Room maid
441.98 Trainee
441.99 Other housekeepers, maids and related personal service occupations

442 Stewards and Attendants (Travel and Transport Services)

442.10 Steward (seagoing)
442.20 Air steward
442.30 Sleeping-car attendant
442.40 Travel courier
442.98 Trainee
442.99 Other stewards and attendants (travel and transport services)

443 Ward Orderlies and Medical Attendants

443.10 Operating theatre attendant
443.20 Ambulanceman
443.30 First aid attendant
443.40 Hospital ward orderly
443.50 Attendant (residential establishment for the elderly or infirm)
443.98 Trainee
443.99 Other ward orderlies and medical attendants

449 Porters and Attendants and Housekeepers and Related Personal Service Occupations Not Elsewhere Classified

449.10 Hall porter (day) (hotel or residential establishment)
449.20 Night porter (hotel or residential establishment)
449.30 Hospital porter
449.50 Page boy (hotel or residential establishment)
449.98 Trainee
449.99 Other porters and attendants and housekeepers and related personal service occupations not elsewhere classified

45 Caretaking, Cleaning and Attending Occupations (Premises and Property)

450 Supervisors and Foremen (Caretaking, Cleaning and Attending Occupations (Premises and Property))

450.10 Supervisor (cleaners)
450.20 Station foreman

450 .30 Supervisor (attendants (premises and property) not elsewhere classified)
450 .98 Trainee
450 .99 Other supervisors (caretaking, cleaning and attending occupations (premises and property))

451 Caretakers
451 .10 Caretaker (church)
451 .20 Caretaker (premises excluding church)

452 Cleaners
452 .10 Cleaner (domestic, public, business premises)
452 .20 Cleaner (workshop, depot, yard)
452 .30 Cleaner (public transport interiors)
452 .40 Window cleaner
452 .50 Chimney sweep
452 .60 Road sweeper
452 .99 Other cleaners

453 Stationmen (Railway)
453 .10 Railman, Stationman
453 .20 Ticket collector (railway)
453 .98 Trainee

459 Attendants (Premises and Property) Not Elsewhere Classified
459 .05 Swimming pool attendant
459 .10 Bath attendant (slipper, remedial, Turkish)
459 .15 Attendant (theatre, cinema, entertainment hall)
459 .20 Doorman
459 .25 Fair ground attendant
459 .30 Lift attendant
459 .35 Cloakroom attendant, Left luggage attendant
459 .40 Lavatory attendant
459 .45 Road vehicle parking attendant
459 .50 Public lighting attendant
459 .55 Bill poster
459 .60 Ticket collector (not elsewhere classified)
459 .98 Trainee
459 .99 Other attendants (premises and property) not elsewhere classified

46 Laundering, Dry Cleaning and Pressing Occupations

460 Supervisors (Laundering, Dry Cleaning and Pressing Occupations)
460 .10 Supervisor (laundering, dry cleaning and pressing occupations)
460 .98 Trainee

461 Laundering, Dry Cleaning and Pressing Occupations
461 .02 Launderer (general)
461 .04 Dry cleaner (general)
461 .06 Dry cleaning machine operator
461 .08 Hand presser (garments)
461 .10 Machine presser (garments)
461 .12 Under presser (hand)
461 .14 Under presser (machine)
461 .16 Ironer
461 .18 Launderette assistant
461 .50 Fur cleaner
461 .55 Machine washer
461 .60 Hydro-extractor operator
461 .65 Tumbler operator
461 .70 Calender hand
461 .98 Trainee
461 .99 Other laundering, dry cleaning and pressing occupations

47 Hairdressing and Miscellaneous Service Occupations

470 Supervisors (Hairdressing and Miscellaneous Service Occupations)
470 .10 Supervisor (hairdressers)
470 .20 Funeral director
470 .30 Assistant superintendent (cemetery, crematorium)
470 .40 Bookmaker
470 .98 Trainee
470 .99 Other supervisors (miscellaneous service occupations)

471 Hairdressing and Beauty Treatment Occupations
471 .05 Ladies' hairdresser
471 .10 Men's hairdresser
471 .15 Beautician
471 .20 Make-up artist
471 .50 Wig dresser
471 .60 Manicurist, Pedicurist
471 .98 Trainee
471 .99 Other hairdressing and beauty treatment occupations

472 Burial and Related Service Occupations
472 .10 Embalmer
472 .20 Funeral director's assistant
472 .30 Mortuary attendant
472 .98 Trainee
472 .99 Other burial and related service occupations

479 Miscellaneous Service Occupations Not Elsewhere Classified
479 .05 Croupier
479 .10 Property master
479 .15 Taxidermist
479 .50 Store guide
479 .55 Bingo caller
479 .60 Pest control operator
479 .65 Disinfecting officer
479 .98 Trainee
479 .99 Other miscellaneous service occupations not elsewhere classified

Major Group XI FARMING, FISHING, AND RELATED OCCUPATIONS

50 Farming, Horticultural, Forestry and Related Occupations

500 Foremen (Farming, Horticultural, Forestry and Related Occupations)
500.10 Foreman (arable crop workers)
500.20 Foreman (mixed farming workers)
500.30 Foreman (farm livestock workers)
500.40 Foreman (animal workers other than farm livestock workers)
500.50 Foreman (horticultural workers)
500.60 Foreman (gardeners and groundsmen)
500.70 Foreman (agricultural machinery operators)
500.80 Foreman (tree cultivating and harvesting workers)
500.98 Trainee
500.99 Other foremen (farming, horticultural, forestry and related occupations)

501 Farm Workers (Arable and Mixed Farming)
501.10 Agricultural worker (general) (arable crops)
501.20 Agricultural worker (hand) (arable crops)
501.30 Agricultural worker (hop gardens)
501.40 Agricultural worker (mixed farming)
501.98 Trainee
501.99 Other farm workers (arable and mixed farming)

502 Animal Tending and Breeding Occupations
502.02 Stockman (mixed farm livestock)
502.04 Cowman
502.06 Stockman (beef cattle)
502.08 Stockman (sheep)
502.10 Stockman (pigs)
502.12 Attendant (domestic or working animals except farm livestock and horses)
502.14 Attendant (wild animals)
502.16 Attendant (horses)
502.18 Gamekeeper
502.20 Beekeeper
502.22 Mink farm assistant
502.24 Inseminator
502.50 Poultryman
502.60 Hatchery worker
502.98 Trainee
502.99 Other animal tending and breeding occupations

503 Horticultural Workers
503.10 Glasshouse worker
503.20 Nursery worker (excluding glasshouse worker)
503.30 Market garden worker (excluding glasshouse worker)
503.40 Orchard worker
503.98 Trainee
503.99 Other horticultural workers

504 Gardeners and Groundsmen
504.10 Gardener (public gardens)
504.20 Gardener (private gardens)
504.30 Landscape gardener
504.40 Turf layer
504.50 Groundsman
504.98 Trainee
504.99 Other gardeners and groundsmen

505 Agricultural Machinery Operators
505.10 Agricultural machinery operator
505.98 Trainee

506 Tree Cultivating and Harvesting Occupations
506.10 Forest worker (excluding nursery worker)
506.50 Tree feller (trimming, felling)
506.98 Trainee
506.99 Other tree cultivating and harvesting occupations

509 Farming, Horticultural, Forestry and Related Occupations Not Elsewhere Classified
509.10 Classifier and marker (farm livestock)
509.50 Hedger
509.90 Crop harvester
509.98 Trainee
509.99 Other farming, horticultural, forestry and related occupations not elsewhere classified

51 Fishing and Related Occupations

510 Supervisors and Mates (Fishing and Related Occupations)
510.10 Mate (fishing vessel)
510.20 Third hand (fishing vessel)
510.99 Other supervisors and mates (fishing and related occupations)

511 Fishermen
511.10 Fisherman (deck hand)
511.20 Pot fisherman
511.98 Trainee
511.99 Other fishermen

519 Fishing and Related Occupations Not Elsewhere Classified
519.10 Shellfish cultivator
519.20 Fish hatcher
519.98 Trainee
519.99 Other fishing and related occupations not elsewhere classified

Major Group XII MATERIALS PROCESSING OCCUPATIONS (EXCLUDING METAL)

53 Hide, Skin and Pelt Processing Occupations

530 Foremen (Hide, Skin and Pelt Processing Occupations)
530.10 Foreman (hide, skin and pelt processing occupations)
530.98 Trainee

531 Hide, Skin and Pelt Processing Occupations
531.10 Limeyard worker (general), Fellmonger (general)
531.20 Wool puller and sorter (hand)
531.30 Splitting machine operator
531.50 Fleshing machine operator. Unhairing machine operator, Scouring machine operator
531.55 Cutter
531.60 Tanyard handler
531.65 Drum operator
531.70 Finisher (machine)
531.90 Trimmer
531.91 De-Wooling machine operator
531.92 Drying room operative, Conditioning room operative
531.93 Pelt dressing machine operator
531.98 Trainee
531.99 Other hide, skin and pelt processing occupations

54 Fibre and Textile Processing and Fabric Making Occupations

540 Foremen (Fibre and Textile Processing and Fabric Making Occupations)
540.05 Foreman (fibre preparing occupations)
540.10 Foreman (textile spinning occupations)
540.15 Foreman (textile doubling, twisting, winding occupations)
540.20 Foreman (warp preparing occupations)
540.25 Foreman (textile weaving occupations)
540.30 Foreman (knitting occupations)
540.35 Foreman (textile bleaching, finishing and other treating occupations) (excluding dyeing)
540.40 Foreman (textile dyeing occupations)
540.45 Foreman (textile repairing occupations)
540.50 Foreman (braid, plait, line and fibre rope making occupations)
540.55 Foreman (pattern card and tape preparing occupations)
540.60 Foreman (felt hood making occupations)
540.98 Trainee
540.99 Other foremen (fibre and textile processing and fabric making occupations)

541 Fibre Preparing Occupations
541.05 Fibre mixer and blender (machine)
541.10 Fibre separating and aligning machine operator
541.15 Drawframe attendant, Speed frame attendant
541.20 Gill box attendant, Drawing box attendant
541.25 Tow-to-top converter attendant
541.30 Flagger
541.50 Fibre opening machine attendant
541.55 Fibre separating and aligning machine attendant
541.60 Fibre cutter
541.65 Rag ripper and cutter
541.70 Waste cutting machine attendant, Waste grinding machine attendant
541.98 Trainee
541.99 Other fibre preparing occupations

542 Textile Spinning, Doubling, Twisting and Winding Occupations
542.10 Mule spinner
542.50 Assistant mule spinner
542.55 Frame spinner
542.60 Spinner (metal thread)
542.65 Assembly winder
542.70 Twister
542.75 Yarn texturer
542.80 Winder, Reeler
542.90 Baller (machine), Spooler (machine)
542.92 Card winder
542.98 Trainee
542.99 Other textile spinning, doubling, twisting and winding occupations

543 Warp Preparing Occupations
543.05 Warp sizer
543.10 Drawer-in (hand)
543.15 Drawing machine setter
543.20 Healding machine operator
543.25 Warp twister-in
543.30 Warp threader (warp knitting)
543.50 Warper (machine)
543.55 Drawing machine operator
543.60 Warp pinning machine operator
543.65 Setter (spool Axminster carpet)
543.70 Threader (spool Axminster carpet)
543.90 Reacher-in
543.98 Trainee
543.99 Other warp preparing occupations

544 Textile Weaving Occupations
544.05 Carpet weaver (power loom)
544.10 Fabric weaver (power loom)
544.15 Hand loom weaver (fabric)

544 .20 Pattern weaver
544 .25 Smash hand
544 .30 Lace weaver
544 .50 Netting weaver
544 .98 Trainee
544 .99 Other textile weaving occupations

545 Knitting Occupations

545 .10 Flat machine knitter (hand)
545 .20 Flat machine knitter (power)
545 .50 Circular machine knitter
545 .60 Warp knitter
545 .70 Bar filler
545 .98 Trainee
545 .99 Other knitting occupations

546 Textile Bleaching, Dyeing, Finishing and Other Treating Occupations

546 .10 Molten metal dyeing machine operator
546 .20 Re-dyer
546 .50 Backwash attendant
546 .52 Bleacher
546 .54 Operative dyer
546 .56 Finishing solution tank operator
546 .58 Miller
546 .60 Continuous textile finishing unit operator
546 .62 Singeing machine operator
546 .64 Stenterer
546 .66 Shrinking machine operator
546 .68 Cropper (fabric, carpet)
546 .70 Flat presser
546 .72 Raiser
546 .74 Boarder
546 .85 Carboniser
546 .86 Washer, automatic scouring machine attendant
546 .87 Dipper
546 .88 Crabber
546 .89 Drier, Hydro-extractor operator
546 .90 Damper
546 .91 Calenderer
546 .92 Blower
546 .93 Clipper (cordage)
546 .98 Trainee
546 .99 Other textile bleaching, dyeing, finishing and treating occupations

547 Textile Repairing Occupations

547 .10 Mender (woven piece goods)
547 .20 Invisible mender (repair service)
547 .30 Net repairer
547 .50 Burler (cloth)
547 .55 Mender (carpet, rug)
547 .60 Mender (fibre hose-pipe)
547 .65 Mender (hosiery, knitwear)
547 .70 Mender (lace)
547 .75 Net examiner and finisher
547 .98 Trainee
547 .99 Other textile repairing occupations

548 Braid, Plait, Line and Fibre Rope Making Occupations

548 .10 Rope maker (rope-walk)
548 .50 Rope maker's assistant
548 .55 Line maker, Twine maker
548 .60 Rope layer (house machine)
548 .65 Twisting machine operator
548 .70 Braiding machine attendant
548 .90 Bullion cord covering machinist
548 .92 Bullion cord maker
548 .98 Trainee
548 .99 Other braid, plait, line and fibre rope making occupations

549 Fibre and Textile Processing and Fabric Making Occupations Not Elsewhere Classified

549 .02 Colour matcher
549 .04 Harness builder
549 .06 Pattern card cutter
549 .08 Pattern card corrector
549 .10 Pattern card repeater operator
549 .12 Coating machine operator
549 .14 Combining machine operator
549 .16 Fuller
549 .18 Fur felt hood former
549 .20 Wool felt hood former
549 .50 Fibre preparing and spinning set attendant
549 .51 Chain maker (loom)
549 .52 Chain maker (warp knitting machine)
549 .53 Fibre bonding machine operator
549 .54 Tufting machine operator
549 .55 Needleloom operator
549 .56 Typewriter ribbon inker
549 .57 Net maker (hand), Braider
549 .58 Net fixer
549 .59 Splicer (fibre rope)
549 .60 Felter (mechanical cloth)
549 .61 Felt hood hardening machine operator
549 .62 Felt hood shrinking machine attendant
549 .63 Rope coiler (machine)
549 .64 Warp splitter
549 .65 Dyer's preparer
549 .85 Hair fibre preparing and spinning machine attendant
549 .86 Fibre batt hardening machine operator
549 .87 Creeler, Battery filler
549 .88 Doffer
549 .89 Warp doubler
549 .90 Lapper (machine), Winder (machine)
549 .91 Fabric opening machine attendant
549 .92 Fur fibre mixer
549 .93 Pattern card lacer
549 .98 Trainee
549 .99 Other fibre and textile processing and fabric making occupations not elsewhere classified

55 Tobacco Processing and Products Making Occupations

550 Foremen (Tobacco Processing and Products Making Occupations)

550 .10 Foreman (tobacco processing and products making occupations)
550 .98 Trainee

551 Tobacco Processing and Products Making Occupations

551.10	Drier
551.20	Cigarette making machine operator
551.50	Leaf conditioner
551.55	Stemmer (hand)
551.60	Cutting machine operator
551.65	Roll spinner
551.70	Cigar machinist
551.90	Stemmer (machine), Threshing machine attendant
551.91	Machine feeder
551.92	Press operator
551.98	Trainee
551.99	Other tobacco processing and products making occupations

56 Chemical, Gas and Petroleum Processing Plant Operating Occupations

560 Supervisors (Chemical, Gas and Petroleum Processing Plant Operating Occupations)

560.10	Supervisor (chemical, gas and petroleum processing plant operating occupations)
560.98	Trainee

561 Chemical, Gas and Petroleum Processing Plant Operating Occupations

561.05	Chief operator
561.10	Senior operator
561.15	Continuous plant operator
561.20	Batch plant operator (general)
561.50	Batch plant operator (heat treating, chemical reaction)
561.60	Batch plant operator (crushing, milling, mixing, blending)
561.70	Batch plant operator (filtering, straining and other mechanical separating)
561.98	Trainee
561.99	Other chemical, gas and petroleum processing plant operating occupations

57 Food and Drink Processing Occupations

570 Foremen (Food and Drink Processing Occupations)

570.10	Foreman (bakers and flour confectioners)
570.20	Foreman (slaughtermen, butchers and meat cutters)
570.30	Foreman (fish preparers, poultry dressers)
570.40	Foreman (cooking, freezing and other heat treating occupations) (food and drink processing)
570.50	Foreman (crushing, milling, mixing and blending occupations) (food and drink processing)
570.60	Foreman (filtering, straining and other separating occupations) (food and drink processing)
570.70	Foreman (plant and machine operating occupations (food and drink processing) not elsewhere classified)
570.98	Trainee
570.99	Other foremen (food and drink processing occupations)

571 Bakers and Flour Confectioners

571.05	Bread baker
571.10	Flour confectioner
571.15	Baker and confectioner
571.20	Hand decorator (flour confectionery)
571.50	Table hand (bakery)
571.98	Trainee
571.99	Other bakers and flour confectioners

572 Meat, Fish and Poultry Slaughtering and Preparing Occupations

572.10	Slaughterman
572.20	Butcher
572.30	Meat cutter
572.50	Poultry dresser
572.60	Fish preparer (hand)
572.90	Fish preparer (machine)
572.98	Trainee
572.99	Other meat, fish and poultry slaughtering and preparing occupations

573 Cooking, Freezing and Other Heat Treating Occupations (Food and Drink Processing)

573.05	Sugar boiler (sugar refining)
573.10	Continuous cooker operator (jam)
573.15	Refiner (chocolate)
573.20	Kilnman maltster
573.25	Malt roaster
573.50	Drying plant operator
573.52	Evaporator operator
573.54	Cooker (fruit, vegetables, meat, fish)
573.56	Tripe and feet dresser
573.58	Cheese cook (processed cheese manufacture)
573.60	Sugar boiler (sugar confectionery manufacture)
573.62	Inversion attendant
573.64	Roaster (dextrin)
573.66	Mash room man
573.68	Copperhead worker
573.70	Butter liquefier (margarine manufacture)
573.72	Ovensman (bread, flour confectionery)
573.74	Roaster (nuts, beans, chicory)
573.76	Smoker (foodstuffs)
573.78	Retort operator (canned, bottled foodstuffs)
573.80	Cooling equipment operator
573.90	Sugar boiler (syrup manufacture)
573.91	Crystalliser attendant (sugar candy manufacture)
573.92	Steriliser (milk, ice cream)
573.93	Blancher (fruit, vegetables)

573.94 Freezer operator
573.95 Ice room attendant
573.98 Trainee
573.99 Other cooking, freezing and heat treating occupations (food and drink processing)

574 Crushing, Milling, Mixing and Blending Occupations (Food and Drink Processing)

574.10 Rollerman (flour milling)
574.50 Rollerman (foodstuffs excluding flour)
574.52 Grinding machine operator (foodstuffs)
574.54 Mixer (bread and flour confectionery)
574.56 Mixerman (compound animal food)
574.58 Compounder (soft drinks, wines, ciders, liqueurs, spirits)
574.60 Butter blender
574.62 Concher (chocolate)
574.90 Millhand (fruit pulping)
574.91 Nut processing machine operator
574.92 Mixer (not elsewhere classified)
574.93 Seed tank man (yeast)
574.94 Viscoliser operator (ice cream), Homogeniser operator (ice cream)
574.98 Trainee
574.99 Other crushing, milling, mixing and blending occupations (food and drink processing)

575 Filtering, Straining and Other Separating Occupations (Food and Drink Processing)

575.10 Butter churn operator
575.50 Filter press operator
575.55 Rotary drum filter operator
575.60 Centrifuge operator
575.65 Sieve operator
575.90 Diffuser attendant, Diffuser battery hand
575.98 Trainee
575.99 Other filtering, straining and separating occupations (food and drink processing)

576 Plant and Machine Operating Occupations (Food and Drink Processing) Not Elsewhere Classified

576.05 Ice cream maker
576.10 Chocolate maker
576.15 Utility operator (maize starch, animal food)
576.20 Cheese maker (excluding processed cheese)
576.25 Macaroni making equipment operator
576.30 Screensman conditioner (grain, seed)
576.50 Setter-operator (bakery equipment)
576.52 Shredding machine operator (cereals)
576.54 Coating equipment operator (confectionery)

576.56 Machine moulder (chocolate)
576.58 Acidifier operator (dextrin)
576.60 Dairy worker (margarine)
576.62 Votator operator (edible fat manufacture)
576.64 Cube sugar equipment operator
576.66 Barrelman (rice starch)
576.68 Steep operator (maize starch)
576.70 Wet mill operator (maize starch)
576.72 Oil extractor (grain germ, seed oil extraction)
576.74 Carbonatation man
576.76 Carbonation and filtration man (ciders, wines)
576.85 Automatic equipment attendant
576.86 Sugar beet cutter
576.87 Cutting machine operator (sugar confectionery)
576.88 Mogul operator (sugar confectionery)
576.89 Fondant machine operator
576.90 Liquorice extruding machine operator
576.91 Shell separation machine operator (cocoa beans)
576.92 Drying room hand (rice starch)
576.93 Skin filling machine operator (meat products)
576.98 Trainee
576.99 Other plant and machine operating occupations (food and drink processing) not elsewhere classified

579 Food and Drink Processing Occupations Not Elsewhere Classified

579.05 Slab hand (sugar confectionery)
579.10 Hand moulder (chocolate, sugar confectionery)
579.15 Hand dipper (chocolate confectionery)
579.20 Piper (chocolate, sugar confectionery)
579.25 Fermentation man (brewing, whisky distilling)
579.30 Vatman (cider, wine)
579.35 Briner, Dry salter
579.50 Floorman maltster
579.55 Racker (brewing)
579.60 Preparer (hand) (fruit, vegetables)
579.65 Operative's helper (food, drink processing) (not elsewhere classified)
579.98 Trainee
579.99 Other food and drink processing occupations not elsewhere classified

58 Wood Processing and Paper, Paperboard and Leatherboard Making Occupations

580 Foremen (Wood Processing and Paper, Paperboard and Leatherboard Making Occupations)

580.10 Foreman (heat treating occupations (wood processing and paper, paperboard and leatherboard making))

580 .20 Foreman (crushing, milling, mixing and blending occupations (wood processing and paper, paperboard and leatherboard making))

580 .30 Foreman (filtering, straining and other separating occupations (wood processing and paper, paperboard and leatherboard making))

580 .40 Foreman (plant and machine operating occupations (wood processing and paper, paperboard and leatherboard making) not elsewhere classified)

580 .98 Trainee

580 .99 Other foremen (wood processing and paper, paperboard and leatherboard making occupations)

581 Heat Treating Occupations (Wood Processing and Paper, Paperboard and Leatherboard Making)

581 .10 Kiln drier (wood)

581 .50 Drier operator (wood, paper)

581 .98 Trainee

581 .99 Other heat treating occupations (wood processing and paper, paperboard and leatherboard making)

582 Crushing, Milling, Mixing and Blending Occupations (Wood Processing and Paper, Paperboard and Leatherboard Making)

582 .10 Beaterman (paper making)

582 .50 Beaterman (leatherboard)

582 .60 Pulper

582 .90 Wood mill attendant

582 .98 Trainee

582 .99 Other crushing, milling, mixing and blending occupations (wood processing and paper, paperboard and leatherboard making)

583 Filtering, Straining and Other Separating Occupations (Wood Processing and Paper, Paperboard and Leatherboard Making)

583 .10 Up-taking machine operator

583 .98 Trainee

583 .99 Other filtering, straining and separating occupations (wood processing and paper, paperboard and leatherboard making)

584 Plant and Machine Operating Occupations (Wood Processing and Paper, Paperboard and Leatherboard Making) Not Elsewhere Classified

584 .05 Paper making machineman, Paperboard making machineman

584 .10 Drierman (paper making machine), Drierman (paperboard making machine)

584 .15 Coating machine operator (paper, paperboard), Impregnating machine operator (paper, paperboard)

584 .20 Combining machine operator (paper, paperboard)

584 .50 Paper making machine assistant, Paperboard making machine assistant

584 .55 Coating machine assistant (paper, paperboard), Impregnating machine assistant (paper, paperboard)

584 .60 Combining machine assistant (paper, paperboard)

584 .65 Calender operator

584 .70 Leatherboard making machine operator

584 .75 Laminator (power press)

584 .80 Winder operator

584 .90 Plant attendant (wood processing and paper, paperboard and leatherboard making) not elsewhere classified, Machine attendant (wood processing and paper, paperboard and leatherboard making) not elsewhere classified

584 .98 Trainee

584 .99 Other plant and machine operating occupations (wood processing and paper, paperboard and leatherboard making) not elsewhere classified

589 Wood Processing and Paper, Paperboard and Leatherboard Making Occupations Not Elsewhere Classified

589 .10 Paper maker (hand)

589 .50 Combiner (hand) (paper, paperboard)

589 .90 Layer

589 .98 Trainee

589 .99 Other wood processing and paper, paperboard and leatherboard making occupations not elsewhere classified

59 Materials Processing Occupations Not Elsewhere Classified

590 Foremen (Materials Processing Occupations Not Elsewhere Classified)

590 .10 Foreman (heat treating occupations not elsewhere classified)

590 .20 Foreman (crushing, milling, mixing and blending occupations not elsewhere classified)

590 .30 Foreman (filtering, straining and other mechanical separating occupations not elsewhere classified)

590 .40 Foreman (plant and machine operating occupations (materials processing) not elsewhere classified)

590 .98 Trainee

590 .99 Other foremen (materials processing occupations not elsewhere classified)

591 Heat Treating Occupations Not Elsewhere Classified

591 .10 Furnaceman (glass making)

591 .20 Kiln burner (cement)

591 .50 Furnaceman (vitreous silica)

591.52 Assistant furnaceman (vitreous silica)

591.54 Safety glass toughener

591.56 Roaster (not elsewhere classified)

591.58 Kiln operator (ceramic products)

591.60 Kiln operator (abrasive, carbon products)

591.62 Drier and kiln attendant

591.64 Drier operator (plasterboard)

591.66 Autoclave operator (mineral products)

591.68 Cooker (not elsewhere classified)

591.70 Belt pressman

591.90 Annealing equipment attendant (glass, glassware), Toughening equipment attendant (glass)

591.92 Heat treatment equipment attendant (not elsewhere classified)

591.98 Trainee

591.99 Other heat treating occupations not elsewhere classified

592 Crushing, Milling, Mixing and Blending Occupations Not Elsewhere Classified

592.05 Colour calculator

592.10 Colour matcher

592.15 Liquor man (leather tanning)

592.20 Dough preparer (artificial teeth)

592.25 Slip maker (ceramics), Glaze maker

592.50 Mineral crushing plant operator

592.55 Masticating millman

592.60 Miller (not elsewhere classified)

592.65 Beaterman (asbestos-cement)

592.70 Rubber compounder, Rubber mixer

592.75 Mixing machine operator (not elsewhere classified), Blending machine operator (not elsewhere classified)

592.90 Crushing plant attendant (not elsewhere classified), Mill attendant (not elsewhere classified)

592.92 Mixing machine attendant (not elsewhere classified), Blending machine attendant (not elsewhere classified)

592.98 Trainee

592.99 Other crushing, milling, mixing and blending occupations not elsewhere classified

593 Filtering, Straining and Other Mechanical Separating Occupations Not Elsewhere Classified

593.05 Flotation plant operator

593.10 Heavy media plant operator

593.15 Magnetic separator operator

593.20 Filter press operator (not elsewhere classified)

593.25 Rotary drum filter operator (not elsewhere classified)

593.30 Centrifuge operator (not elsewhere classified)

593.35 Siever (not elsewhere classified)

593.40 Sedimentation plant operator (not elsewhere classified)

593.45 Sewage works attendant

593.98 Trainee

593.99 Other filtering, straining and mechanical separating occupations not elsewhere classified

594 Plant and Machine Operating Occupations (Materials Processing) Not Elsewhere Classified

594.10 Machine man (flat asbestos-cement sheet making)

594.20 Machine man (asbestos-cement pipe making)

594.50 Machine man (corrugated asbestos-cement sheet making)

594.52 Corrugator (asbestos-cement sheet)

594.54 Assistant machine man (asbestos-cement sheet, pipe making)

594.56 Plasterboard making machine operator

594.58 Man-made fibre maker

594.60 Calender operator (rubber, plastics)

594.62 Extruding machine operator (rubber, plastics)

594.64 Coating machine operator (film, recording tape)

594.90 Calenderer (asbestos composition)

594.92 Materials processing plant attendant (not elsewhere classified), Materials processing machine attendant (not elsewhere classified)

594.98 Trainee

594.99 Other plant and machine operating occupations (materials processing) not elsewhere classified

599 Other Materials Processing Occupations

599.10 Kiln placer

599.50 Kiln setter

599.60 Hand moulder (not elsewhere classified)

599.70 Mica splitter (hand)

599.90 Impregnator (immersion) (not elsewhere classified)

599.98 Trainee

599.99 Other materials processing occupations not elsewhere classified

Major Group XIII MAKING AND REPAIRING OCCUPATIONS (EXCLUDING METAL AND ELECTRICAL)

61 Glass Working Occupations

610 Foremen (Glass Working Occupations)

610.10 Foreman (glass shaping and forming occupations (hand) (excluding optical glass))

610.20 Foreman (glass shaping and forming occupations (machine) (excluding optical glass))

610.30 Foreman (optical glass shaping, forming and finishing occupations)

610.40 Foreman (glass finishing occupations (excluding optical glass and painting))

610.98 Trainee

610.99 Other foremen (glass working occupations)

611 Glass Shaping and Forming Occupations (Hand) (Excluding Optical Glass)

611.05 Chairman, Servitor

611.10 Glass blower (mould)

611.15 Crown glass maker

611.20 Glass tube maker (hand drawing), Glass rod maker (hand drawing)

611.25 Glass tube bender (neon signs)

611.30 Glass bench worker

611.50 Footmaker

611.60 Glass bender

611.70 Piece opener

611.98 Trainee

611.99 Other glass shaping and forming occupations (hand) (excluding optical glass)

612 Glass Shaping and Forming Occupations (Machine) (Excluding Optical Glass)

612.10 Glass presser

612.20 Cut-off man (sheet glass)

612.30 Glass tube maker (machine), Glass rod maker (machine)

612.50 Glass lathe worker

612.55 Balcony man (vertical lehr)

612.60 Glass tube cutter

612.65 Glass driller

612.70 Automatic bottle making machine operator

612.75 Tank operator (flat glass)

612.98 Trainee

612.99 Other glass shaping and forming occupations (machine) (excluding optical glass)

613 Optical Glass Shaping, Forming and Finishing Occupations

613.05 Moulder

613.10 Optical slab grinder and polisher

613.15 Optical element worker (hand)

613.20 Optical element smoother and polisher (machine)

613.25 Lens surfacing machine operator

613.30 Smoother (ophthalmic prescription)

613.35 Hand glazer

613.40 Hand edger

613.50 Selector

613.55 Optical glass lump grinder

613.60 Glass milling machine setter-operator

613.65 Smoother (ophthalmic stock)

613.70 Polisher (ophthalmic lenses)

613.75 Centerer and edger (optical element)

613.80 Machine glazer and edger

613.90 Remoulder

613.91 Optical slab cutter

613.92 Optical glass cutter

613.93 Rougher (hand)

613.94 Roughing machine attendant

613.95 Optical element smoother (machine)

613.96 Optical element polisher (machine)

613.98 Trainee

613.99 Other optical glass shaping, forming and finishing occupations

614 Glass Finishing Occupations (Excluding Optical Glass and Painting)

614.05 Decorative cutter (manual)

614.10 Acid embosser (glass decorating)

614.15 Abrasive etcher (glass decorating)

614.20 Edge finisher (flat glass)

614.25 Surface polisher (flat glass)

614.50 Badger (glass decorating)

614.55 Marker-out (glass decorating)

614.60 Cutter (hand wheel) (glass decorating)

614.65 Hand grinder

614.70 Machine grinder

614.75 Acid polisher (glass)

614.80 Burner-off, Cracker-off

614.90 Pattern cutting machine operator (glass decorating)

614.91 Sandblasting machine operator (glass decorating)

614.92 Acid bath attendant (glass frosting)

614.93 Fire polisher (glassware), Melter (glassware)

614.98 Trainee

614.99 Other glass finishing occupations (excluding optical glass and painting)

619 Glass Working Occupations Not Elsewhere Classified

619.10 Lens marker-up (ophthalmic prescription)

619.20 Rimless driller and fitter (spectacles)

619.30 Glass cutter (flat glass)

619.50 Gatherer (glass making)

619.55 Laminated glass worker

619.60 Plant operator (glass fibre tissue)

619.65 Sprayman operator (glass fibre wool plant)
619.70 Plant operator (continuous glass fibre filament)
619.75 Plant operator (chopped glass fibre mat)
619.90 Knocker-off (lens)
619.92 Breaker-off (sheet glass)
619.98 Trainee
619.99 Other glass working occupations not elsewhere classified

62 Clay and Stone Working Occupations

620 Foreman (Clay and Stone Working Occupations)

620.10 Foreman (ceramic goods forming occupations)
620.20 Foreman (ceramic goods finishing occupations (excluding glazers and decorators))
620.30 Foreman (concrete, asbestos-cement, abrasive stone and related products making occupations)
620.40 Foreman (stone cutting, shaping and polishing occupations)
620.98 Trainee
620.99 Other foremen (clay and stone working occupations)

621 Ceramic Goods Forming Occupations

621.02 Modeller (pottery, porcelain)
621.04 Plaster mould maker
621.06 Thrower (pottery, porcelain)
621.08 Hand turner (pottery, stoneware)
621.10 Jollier, Jiggerer
621.12 Glasshouse pot maker
621.14 Saggar maker (hand)
621.16 Hand presser (pottery), Hand moulder (stoneware, refractory goods)
621.18 Caster (pottery, refractory)
621.20 Caster (plaster)
621.22 Crucible maker (machine)
621.24 Brick maker (machine)
621.26 Sanitary mason
621.28 Furnace moulder
621.50 Ornamenter (pottery, porcelain)
621.52 Turning machine minder (pottery, earthenware)
621.54 Jolley machine minder, Jigger machine minder
621.56 Hand moulder (bricks, roofing tiles)
621.58 Press operator (ceramics)
621.60 Extruding press operator (clay)
621.62 Chequerer (clay building tiles)
621.90 Automatic press minder (ceramics)
621.92 Machine attendant (brick, tile making)
621.98 Trainee
621.99 Other ceramic goods forming occupations

622 Ceramic Goods Finishing Occupations (Excluding Glazers and Decorators)

622.05 Fettler (ceramic goods)
622.10 Grinder (pottery, porcelain), Polisher (pottery, porcelain)
622.15 Scourer (pottery)
622.20 Sandblaster (pottery)
622.50 Etcher (pottery)
622.55 Etcher's assistant (pottery)
622.60 Filler (pottery)
622.65 Tumbler operator (ceramic components)
622.98 Trainee
622.99 Other ceramic goods finishing occupations (excluding glazers and decorators)

623 Concrete, Asbestos-Cement, Abrasive Stone and Related Products Making Occupations

623.02 Mould maker (asbestos-cement)
623.04 Moulder's cutter (asbestos-cement)
623.06 Hand moulder (asbestos-cement products)
623.08 Moulder (abrasive products)
623.10 Moulder (concrete, cast stone)
623.12 Press moulding machine operator (concrete)
623.14 Moulding machine operator (concrete pipes)
623.16 Spinner (concrete)
623.18 Concrete finisher
623.20 Tile caster (terrazzo, mosaic), Slab caster (terrazzo, mosaic)
623.22 Hone maker
623.24 Turner (asbestos-cement)
623.26 Sawyer (asbestos-cement)
623.28 Trimmer (abrasive wheels)
623.30 Steel shot surfacer (abrasive wheel)
623.32 Balancer (abrasive wheel)
623.50 Plant attendant (concrete tile making)
623.98 Trainee
623.99 Other concrete, asbestos-cement, abrasive stone and related products making occupations

624 Stone Cutting, Shaping and Polishing Occupations

624.02 Block cutter (stone, slate)
624.04 Banker mason
624.06 Monumental mason
624.08 Stone carver
624.10 Letter cutter (hand)
624.12 Letter cutter (machine)
624.14 Stone working machine operator
624.16 Grindstone maker (natural stone)
624.18 Slate cutter
624.50 Slate dresser (machine)
624.55 Stone polisher (hand)
624.60 Stone polisher (machine)
624.65 Polisher (machine) (terrazzo or mosaic tiles or slabs)
624.98 Trainee
624.99 Other stone cutting, shaping and polishing occupations

629 Clay and Stone Working Occupations Not Elsewhere Classified

629.10 Industrial insulator builder
629.20 Junction sticker (vitrified clay goods)
629.50 Pipe jointing operative (vitrified clay pipes)
629.90 Crucible maker's assistant
629.92 Mason's labourer (workshop, yard)
629.98 Trainee
629.99 Other clay and stone working occupations not elsewhere classified

63 Printing, Photographic Processing and Related Occupations

630 Foremen (Printing, Photographic Processing and Related Occupations)

630.10 Foreman (composing and typesetting occupations)
630.20 Foreman (printing plate and cylinder preparing occupations (excluding metal engraving))
630.30 Foreman (printing machine operators (excluding screen and block printing))
630.40 Foreman (screen and block printing occupations)
630.50 Foreman (photographic processing and related occupations)
630.98 Trainee
630.99 Other foremen (printing, photographic processing and related occupations)

631 Printers (General)

631.10 Printer (general)
631.98 Trainee

632 Composing and Typesetting Occupations

632.05 Layout man
632.10 Compositor (hand)
632.15 Compositor (imposition)
632.20 Keyboard operator (typesetting)
632.25 Monotype caster operator
632.30 Compositor (linecasting machine)
632.35 Filmsetting machine operator
632.40 Make-up hand
632.98 Trainee
632.99 Other composing and typesetting occupations

633 Printing Plate and Cylinder Preparing Occupations (Excluding Metal Engraving)

633.02 Stereotyper
633.04 Electrotyper
633.06 Printer on metal (process engraving)
633.08 Printer down (photo-lithography)
633.10 Carbon printer (photogravure)
633.12 Planner (photogravure, photo-lithography)
633.14 Lithographic assistant
633.98 Trainee
633.99 Other printing plate and cylinder preparing occupations (excluding metal engraving)

634 Printing Machine Operators (Excluding Screen and Block Printing)

634.05 Letterpress machine minder (platen press, cylinder press)
634.10 Letterpress machine minder (rotary press)
634.15 Lithographic machine minder
634.20 Photogravure machine minder
634.25 Prover
634.30 Die stamper
634.35 Machine printer (textiles)
634.40 Machine printer (wallpaper)
634.50 Embossing machine operator (wallpaper)
634.55 Embossing machine operator (excluding wallpaper)
634.60 Offset duplicating machine operator
634.65 Upper marker (footwear)
634.98 Trainee
634.99 Other printing press machine operators

635 Screen and Block Printing Occupations

635.05 Screen printer (machine) (excluding fabric)
635.10 Screen printer (hand) (excluding fabric)
635.15 Block printer (fabric)
635.20 Block printer (wallpaper)
635.50 Screen printer (machine) (fabric)
635.60 Screen printer (hand) (fabric)
635.98 Trainee
635.99 Other screen and block printing occupations

636 Photographic Processing and Related Occupations

636.02 Film processor (cine)
636.04 Film printer (cine)
636.06 Sensitometric control assistant
636.08 Grader (cine film)
636.10 Cutting and assembly worker (cine film processing)
636.12 Regenerative machine operator (cine film)
636.14 Retoucher (graphic reproduction)
636.16 Retoucher (photographic)
636.50 Still film processor (manual)
636.55 Still film printer (manual)
636.60 Photographic processing machine operator (still)
636.65 Photographic printing machine operator (still)
636.70 Projection printer
636.75 Photographic finisher
636.98 Trainee
636.99 Other photographic processing and related occupations

639 Printing, Photographic Processing and Related Occupations Not Elsewhere Classified

639.05 Screenmaker (screen printing)
639.10 Screenmaker's assistant (screen printing)
639.15 Machine assistant (die stamping)

639.50 Letterpress machine assistant
639.52 Lithographic machine assistant
639.54 Photogravure machine assistant
639.56 Textile printer's assistant
639.58 Machine printer's assistant (wallpaper)
639.60 Stencil cutter (screen printing)
639.62 Roller changer
639.64 Stamper (pottery)
639.90 Tierer (textile printing)
639.98 Trainee
639.99 Other printing, photographic processing and related occupations not elsewhere classified

64 Bookbinding, Paper Working and Paperboard Products Making Occupations

640 Foremen (Bookbinding, Paper Working and Paperboard Products Making Occupations)

640.10 Foreman (bookbinding)
640.20 Foreman (paper working and paperboard products making occupations)
640.98 Trainee

641 Bookbinding Occupations

641.10 Bookbinder (general)
641.20 Bookbinder (sub-divisional)
641.30 Bindery assistant
641.98 Trainee
641.99 Other bookbinding occupations

642 Paper Working and Paperboard Products Making Occupations

642.05 Machine manager
642.10 Machine setter-operator
642.15 Sample maker
642.20 Spiral-tube winder
642.25 Paper pattern copier
642.30 Pattern grader (footwear)
642.50 Machine operator
642.52 Machine minder
642.54 Cutting machine operator
642.56 Slitting machine operator
642.58 Tape fixer (paper patterns)
642.60 Paper pattern cutting machine operator
642.62 Measurer (paper patterns)
642.64 Roll mounting machine operator (stencils)
642.90 Machine assistant
642.92 Spooler (paper tape, film)
642.98 Trainee
642.99 Other paper working and paperboard products making occupations

65 Textile Materials Working Occupations

650 Foremen (Textile Materials Working Occupations)

650.05 Foreman (tailors)
650.10 Foreman (dressmakers and makers throughout of other light clothing)
650.15 Foreman (upholsterers, mattress makers and related occupations)
650.20 Foreman (milliners)
650.25 Foreman (fur garment cutting and shaping occupations)
650.30 Foreman (pattern makers, markers and cutters) (garments, upholstery and related products)
650.35 Foreman (sewing and embroidering occupations) (hand) (garments, upholstery and related products)
650.40 Foreman (sewing and embroidering occupations) (machine) (garments, upholstery and related products)
650.45 Foreman (hat shaping and finishing occupations)
650.98 Trainee
650.99 Other foremen (textile materials working occupations)

651 Tailors

651.10 Tailor (retail bespoke garments)
651.20 Tailor (wholesale bespoke, ready-made garments)
651.30 Tailor's assistant
651.40 Kilt maker
651.50 Alteration fitter
651.60 Alteration hand
651.98 Trainee
651.99 Other tailors

652 Dressmakers and Makers Throughout of Other Light Clothing

652.10 Dressmaker
652.20 Corset maker
652.30 Alteration fitter
652.40 Alteration hand
652.98 Trainee
652.99 Other dressmakers and makers throughout of light clothing

653 Upholsterers, Mattress Makers and Related Occupations

653.05 Coach trimmer
653.10 Upholsterer (furniture)
653.15 Upholsterer (soft furnishings)
653.20 Mattress maker
653.50 Hood and apron maker
653.60 Mattress filling machine operator
653.98 Trainee
653.99 Other upholsterers, mattress makers and related occupations

654 Milliners

654.10 Milliner
654.98 Trainee

655 Fur Garment Cutting and Shaping Occupations

655.10 Fur garment cutter
655.20 Nailer
655.98 Trainee
655.99 Other fur garment cutting and shaping occupations

656 Pattern Makers, Markers and Cutters (Garments, Upholstery and Related Products)

656 .02 Modeller
656 .04 Fur garment pattern maker and fitter
656 .06 Pattern grader (hand)
656 .08 Marker maker
656 .10 Marker (bespoke tailoring)
656 .12 Cutter (bespoke tailoring)
656 .14 Cutter (made-to-measure light clothing)
656 .16 Lay cutter (garments)
656 .18 Shaper
656 .20 Cutter (leather, skin garments), Fur cutter (gloves)
656 .22 Marker cutter (excluding garments)
656 .24 Lay cutter (excluding garments)
656 .26 Carpet planner
656 .50 Lay cutter's assistant
656 .52 Chopper
656 .54 Trimmer (bespoke tailoring)
656 .56 Trimmings cutter
656 .58 Press cutter (garments)
656 .60 Trimmer (knitwear)
656 .62 Brim rounder
656 .64 Press cutter (excluding garments)
656 .66 Slitter
656 .68 Pattern marker
656 .90 Cross cutter
656 .98 Trainee
656 .99 Other pattern makers, markers and cutters (garments, upholstery and related products)

657 Sewing and Embroidering Occupations (Hand) (Garments, Upholstery and Related Products)

657 .10 Hand sewer (fur garments)
657 .20 Hand embroideress
657 .50 Fabric garment finisher
657 .55 Hand sewer (leather, sheepskin garments)
657 .60 Hand sewer (upholstery)
657 .65 Hand sewer (carpet)
657 .70 Mat binder
657 .75 Umbrella finisher
657 .98 Trainee
657 .99 Other sewing and embroidering occupations (hand) (garments, upholstery and related products)

658 Sewing and Embroidering Occupations (Machine) Garments, Upholstery and Related Products

658 .10 Sewing machinist (general)
658 .20 Fur machinist
658 .30 Embroidery machinist
658 .50 Sewing machinist (heavy clothing)
658 .55 Sewing machinist (light clothing)
658 .60 Linking machinist
658 .65 Sewing machinist (heavy fabric) (excluding clothing)
658 .70 Sewing machinist (light fabric) (excluding clothing)
658 .75 Sewing machinist (carpeting, matting, rugs)

658 .80 Automatic sewing machine attendant
658 .98 Trainee
658 .99 Other sewing and embroidering occupations (machine) (garments, upholstery and related products)

659 Textile Materials Working Occupations Not Elsewhere Classified

659 .05 Felt hat shaping and finishing journeyman
659 .10 Hat blocker (hand)
659 .15 Hat blocker (machine), Fibre helmet blocker
659 .20 Rainproof garment bonder
659 .25 Surgical corset fitter
659 .30 Sailmaker
659 .35 Wig mount maker
659 .40 Carpet layer
659 .50 Brim shaper
659 .52 Felt hat finisher
659 .54 Foundation garment fitter
659 .56 Wire stitching machinist
659 .58 Sack worker (general hand)
659 .60 Powder puff maker
659 .62 Finisher (canvas goods, flags, etc)
659 .64 Embroidery machine operator's assistant
659 .66 Repairer (garments, linen, etc)
659 .68 Embroidery mender
659 .90 Felt hood tip stretcher
659 .98 Trainee
659 .99 Other textile materials working occupations not elsewhere classified

66 Leather Working Occupations

660 Foremen (Leather Working Occupations)

660 .10 Foreman (boot and shoe making (bespoke and surgical) occupations)
660 .20 Foreman (leather cutting occupations)
660 .30 Foreman (lasting occupations (footwear))
660 .40 Foreman (leather goods makers and repairers (excluding boots and shoes))
660 .50 Foreman (leather sewing and stitching occupations)
660 .60 Foreman (boot and shoe repairers)
660 .98 Trainee
660 .99 Other foremen (leather working occupations)

661 Boot and Shoe Making (Bespoke and Surgical) Occupations

661 .05 Boot and shoe maker (bespoke)
661 .10 Surgical footwear maker
661 .15 Upper maker (bespoke, surgical footwear)
661 .20 Surgical footwear bottomer
661 .25 Cork maker (surgical footwear)
661 .30 Heeler (bespoke footwear)
661 .35 Heeler (surgical footwear)
661 .40 Fitter

661.45 Finisher
661.98 Trainee
661.99 Other boot and shoe making (bespoke and surgical) occupations

662 Leather Cutting Occupations

662.05 Hand cutter (footwear)
662.10 Hand cutter (leather goods excluding footwear)
662.15 Grading machine operator
662.20 Welt maker
662.50 Press cutter (footwear)
662.55 Press cutter (leather goods excluding footwear)
662.60 Perforating machinist
662.65 Trimmer (hydraulic, mechanical leather goods)
662.70 Leather cutter (machine) (not elsewhere classified)
662.98 Trainee
662.99 Other leather cutting occupations

663 Lasting Occupations (Footwear)

663.10 Hand laster
663.50 Machine laster
663.55 Bench hand (rubber footwear)
663.60 Veldtschoen toe former
663.65 Insole tacker
663.70 Back tacker
663.90 Jointer
663.92 Examiner
663.98 Trainee
663.99 Other lasting occupations (footwear)

664 Leather Goods Makers and Repairers (Excluding Boots and Shoes)

664.05 Saddler
664.10 Harness maker
664.15 Horse collar maker
664.20 Picker maker, Buffer maker
664.25 Machinery belt maker
664.30 Blocker (hydraulic, mechanical leathers)
664.35 Repairer
664.50 Strap maker
664.60 Blocker (leather products excluding hydraulic, mechanical leathers)
664.70 Beltman
664.98 Trainee
664.99 Other leather goods makers and repairers (excluding boots and shoes)

665 Leather Sewing and Stitching Occupations

665.10 Sewer
665.20 Stitcher (hand) (footwear)
665.30 Stitcher (hand) (leather goods excluding footwear)
665.40 Sewing machinist (footwear)
665.50 Sewing machinist (leather goods excluding footwear)
665.98 Trainee
665.99 Other leather sewing and stitching occupations

666 Boot and Shoe Repairers

666.10 Boot and shoe repairer
666.98 Trainee

669 Leather Working Occupations Not Elsewhere Classified

669.02 Pattern cutter (footwear)
669.04 Pattern cutter (leather goods excluding footwear)
669.06 Die planner (footwear)
669.08 Last builder-up
669.10 Clog maker
669.12 Passer (footwear closing)
669.14 Examiner (footwear finishing)
669.16 Bench hand (leather goods excluding footwear)
669.18 Orthopaedic appliance maker (specialised)
669.20 Roller coverer (textile machine) (general)
669.50 Roller coverer (textile machine) (specialised)
669.52 Blocker (footwear)
669.54 Beader, Turn-over binder
669.56 Pounder (footwear)
669.58 Bottom filler (footwear)
669.60 Scourer (footwear)
669.62 Edge setter
669.64 Finisher (mass produced footwear)
669.66 Footwear cleaner
669.68 Repair preparation hand (footwear manufacture)
669.70 Rectifier (footwear manufacture)
669.90 Waist marker
669.91 Rougher (footwear)
669.92 Welt beater
669.93 Leveller (footwear)
669.94 Polisher (footwear)
669.98 Trainee
669.99 Other leather working occupations not elsewhere classified

67 Woodworking Occupations

670 Foremen (Woodworking Occupations)

670.10 Foreman (carpenters, and carpenters and joiners)
670.20 Foreman cabinet maker
670.30 Foreman (wood fitting and joinery occupations (excluding structural woodworking and cabinet makers))
670.40 Foreman (wood sawing and veneer cutting occupations)
670.50 Foreman (woodworking machine workers)
670.60 Foreman (pattern makers (moulds))
670.98 Trainee
670.99 Other foremen (woodworking occupations)

671 Carpenters, and Carpenters and Joiners (Structural Woodworking)

671.05 Carpenter and joiner
671.10 Carpenter (construction)
671.15 Carpenter (formwork)
671.20 Ship's carpenter
671.25 Stage carpenter
671.30 Fitter (shop, office, exhibition stand)
671.35 Ship joiner
671.40 Boat builder
671.45 Shipwright (wood)

671.98 Trainee
671.99 Other carpenters, and carpenters and joiners (structural woodworking)

672 Cabinet Makers

672.10 Cabinet maker
672.20 Chair maker (wood)
672.30 Piano case fitter
672.98 Trainee
672.99 Other cabinet makers

673 Wood Fitting and Joinery Occupations (Excluding Structural Woodworking and Cabinet Makers)

673.05 Template maker
673.10 Pattern maker (plastics products)
673.15 Loftsman (mould loft)
673.20 Scale model maker
673.25 Wood worker (aircraft)
673.30 Joiner (bench)
673.35 Maker (wooden articles excluding furniture, barrels, crates and packing cases)
673.40 Packing case maker, Crate maker
673.45 Cooper
673.50 Fitter-assembler (sports equipment)
673.55 Orthopaedic appliance maker (specialised)
673.60 Stocker (bespoke guns)
673.98 Trainee
673.99 Other wood fitting and joinery occupations (excluding structural woodworking and cabinet makers)

674 Wood Sawing and Veneer Cutting Occupations

674.10 Wood sawyer (primary reduction)
674.20 Wood sawyer (excluding primary reduction)
674.30 Peeling machine operator, Veneer slicer
674.50 Automatic sawmill attendant
674.98 Trainee
674.99 Other wood sawing and veneer cutting occupations

675 Setters and Setter-Operators (Woodworking Machines)

675.05 Woodcutting machine setter
675.10 Woodcutting machine setter-operator (general)
675.15 Woodcutting machine setter-operator (specialised)
675.20 Spindle woodcutting machine setter-operator
675.25 Wood turning lathe setter-operator
675.50 Debarking machine setter-operator
675.98 Trainee
675.99 Other setters and setter-operators (woodworking machines)

676 Operators and Minders (Woodworking Machines)

676.10 Woodcutting machine operator (general)
676.20 Woodcutting machine operator (specialised)
676.30 Sanding machine operator
676.50 Automatic woodworking machine attendant
676.60 Veneer trimmer
676.98 Trainee
676.99 Other operators and minders (woodworking machines)

677 Pattern Makers (Moulds)

677.10 Pattern maker (general)
677.20 Pattern maker (wood)
677.30 Pattern maker (metal)
677.40 Pattern maker (plastics)
677.98 Trainee
677.99 Other pattern makers (moulds)

679 Woodworking Occupations Not Elsewhere Classified

679.05 Wood carver
679.10 Floor layer (hardwood strips)
679.15 Floor layer (wood blocks, parquet)
679.20 Veneer planner
679.25 Veneer repairer, Plywood repairer
679.50 Bender
679.60 Veneer edge jointer
679.90 Woodworking craftsman's mate
679.92 Woodworking machine operator's assistant
679.94 Polisher (small wooden articles)
679.98 Trainee
679.99 Other woodworking occupations not elsewhere classified

68 Rubber and Plastics Working Occupations

680 Foremen (Rubber and Plastics Working Occupations)

680.10 Foreman (rubber and plastics working occupations)
680.20 Foreman (rubber working occupations)
680.30 Foreman (plastics working occupations)
680.98 Trainee

681 Rubber and Plastics Working Occupations

681.02 Liner (rubber), Coverer (rubber)
681.04 Rubber mould maker
681.06 Tyre builder
681.08 Industrial belting builder
681.10 Rubber caster (printing rollers)
681.12 Artificial eye maker (plastic)
681.14 Orthopaedic appliance maker (specialised) (plastic)
681.16 Spectacle frame maker (plastic), Spectacle frame repairer (plastic)
681.50 Dipper (rubber)
681.52 Rubber moulder
681.54 Glass fibre laminator (hand)
681.56 Cutting machine operator (rubber, plastics)

681 .58 Extruded covering machine operator
681 .60 Press moulding machine operator
681 .62 Finisher (rubber, plastic, glass fibre products)
681 .64 Inspector-rectifier
681 .66 Repairer (electric cable sheathing)
681 .68 Contact lens presser (plastics)
681 .70 Belt winder
681 .72 Hose builder (rubber)
681 .74 Winder (pneumatic tyre components)
681 .76 Pneumatic tyre moulder
681 .78 Tyre restorer
681 .80 Rubber goods builder (not elsewhere classified)
681 .90 Vacuum moulding machine operator
681 .92 Moulding machine attendant
681 .94 Extruded covering machine attendant (rubber, plastics)
681 .96 Tyre repairer
681 .98 Trainee
681 .99 Other rubber and plastics working occupations

69 Making and Repairing Occupations Not Elsewhere Classified

690 Foremen (Making and Repairing Occupations Not Elsewhere Classified)

690 .10 Foreman (musical instrument making and repairing occupations not elsewhere classified)
690 .20 Foreman (surgical appliance makers)
690 .98 Trainee
690 .99 Other foremen (making and repairing occupations not elsewhere classified)

691 Musical Instrument Making and Repairing Occupations Not Elsewhere Classified

691 .05 Musical instrument maker (stringed) (bowed)
691 .10 Musical instrument maker (wood-wind)
691 .15 Musical instrument maker (drums)
691 .20 Organ builder
691 .25 Voicer (organ pipe)
691 .30 Organ tuner
691 .35 Piano tuner
691 .40 Piano repairer
691 .45 Stringer (piano)
691 .50 Action assembler (piano)
691 .55 Piano finisher and regulator
691 .98 Trainee
691 .99 Other musical instrument making and repairing occupations not elsewhere classified

692 Surgical Appliance Makers

692 .10 Orthopaedic appliance maker (general)
692 .20 Dental technician
692 .30 Orthodontic technician
692 .40 Maxillo-facial technician
692 .98 Trainee
692 .99 Other surgical appliance makers

699 Other Making and Repairing Occupations

699 .02 Battery repairer
699 .04 Billiard table fitter
699 .06 Candle maker (hand)
699 .08 Lens fixer (ophthalmic prescription)
699 .10 Musical instrument string maker
699 .12 Racket stringer
699 .14 Reed maker (textile accessories)
699 .16 Roller blind maker, Roller shutter maker
699 .18 Styling modeller (motor vehicles)
699 .20 Wicker products maker
699 .22 Wig maker (general)
699 .50 Wig maker (specialised)
699 .52 Brush maker (hand)
699 .54 Brush maker (machine)
699 .56 Covering machine operator (cable, hose, metal wire, metal strip)
699 .58 Cork cutting machine setter-operator
699 .60 Extrusion press setter (electrode coating)
699 .62 Extrusion press operator (electrode coating)
699 .64 Filler (cartridges, detonators, fireworks)
699 .66 Vacuum drying and impregnating tank attendant
699 .68 Lead paster
699 .70 Felter (printing rollers)
699 .72 Lampshade maker
699 .74 Match making machine operator
699 .76 Machine setter (not elsewhere classified)
699 .78 Exhauster (lamp, valve manufacture)
699 .90 Exhausting machine attendant (lamp, valve manufacture)
699 .91 Venetian blind maker
699 .92 Machine operator (not elsewhere classified), Machine attendant (not elsewhere classified)
699 .93 Product finisher (not elsewhere classified)
699 .98 Trainee
699 .99 Other making and repairing occupations not elsewhere classified

Major Group XIV PROCESSING, MAKING, REPAIRING AND RELATED OCCUPATIONS (METAL AND ELECTRICAL)

71 Metal Processing, Forming and Treating Occupations

710 Foremen (Metal Processing, Forming and Treating Occupations)

710.10 Foreman (furnace operating occupations) (metal processing)
710.20 Foreman (rolling, extruding and drawing occupations) (metal processing)
710.30 Foreman (moulders, coremakers and casters) (metal processing)
710.40 Foreman (forging occupations)
710.50 Foreman (metal plating and coating occupations)
710.60 Foreman (metal annealing and tempering occupations)
710.98 Trainee
710.99 Other foremen (metal processing, forming and treating occupations)

711 Furnace Operating Occupations (Metal Processing)

711.02 Blast furnace keeper (iron)
711.04 Slagger (iron blast furnace)
711.06 Forehand furnaceman (wrought iron manufacture)
711.08 Furnace operator (steel making)
711.10 Furnaceman (copper) non-electrolytic)
711.12 Furnaceman (non-ferrous metal alloy manufacture)
711.14 Cupola man
711.16 Crucible furnaceman (foundry)
711.18 Heater (reheating furnace, soaking pit)
711.50 Stove minder (iron blast furnace)
711.52 Helper (iron blast furnace)
711.54 Underhand furnaceman (wrought iron manufacture)
711.56 Furnace assistant (steel making)
711.58 Furnace assistant (non-ferrous metal alloy manufacture)
711.60 Fireman (zinc vertical retort)
711.62 Blast furnace control room operator (zinc production)
711.64 Condenserman (zinc blast furnace)
711.66 Slagger (zinc blast furnace)
711.68 Bullion melter
711.70 Furnaceman (lead smelting)
711.72 Furnaceman (aluminium) (electrolytic)
711.74 Electrolytic refiner (excluding aluminium)
711.76 Lead softener (non-electrolytic)
711.78 Desilveriser (lead)
711.80 Retort furnaceman (lead refining)
711.90 Cupel man (silver recovery)
711.92 Mixer (steel manufacture)
711.98 Trainee
711.99 Other furnace operating occupations (metal processing)

712 Rolling, Extruding and Drawing Occupations (Metal Processing)

712.05 Roller (primary reduction or hot rolling mill team)
712.10 Roller (cold rolling or temper mill team)
712.15 Piercer (seamless tubes)
712.20 Rollerman (seamless tubes)
712.25 Roller straightener
712.50 Rolling mill assistant (primary reduction or hot rolling mill team)
712.55 Rolling mill assistant (cold rolling or temper mill team)
712.60 Lead press worker
712.65 Extrusion press operator (excluding lead)
712.70 Drawer (tube, rod, bar)
712.75 Wire drawing machinist
712.98 Trainee
712.99 Other rolling, extruding and drawing occupations (metal processing)

713 Moulders, Coremakers and Casters (Metal Processing)

713.05 Moulder (general)
713.10 Bench moulder, Floor moulder
713.15 Pit moulder
713.20 Plate moulder
713.25 Coremaker (hand)
713.30 White metaller
713.35 Teemer (steel making)
713.50 Shell moulder, Shell coremaker
713.52 Machine moulder
713.54 Moulder and coremaker (plaster cast process) (foundry)
713.56 Assembler and caster (plaster cast process) (foundry)
713.58 Pig casting machine operator
713.60 Casting bay helper (steel making)
713.62 Caster (foundry)
713.64 Casting machine operator
713.66 Centrifugal caster
713.68 Gravity die caster
713.70 Pressure die caster
713.72 Investment casting operator
713.90 Leader (abrasive wheel)
713.92 Core making machine operator
713.98 Trainee
713.99 Other moulders, coremakers and casters (metal processing)

714 Forging Occupations

714.05 Drop forger
714.10 Forge hammerman
714.15 Forge pressman
714.20 Blacksmith (general)
714.25 Smith (specialised) (excluding farrier)
714.30 Farrier
714.35 Forger (hand tool, edge tool)
714.50 Forging assistant (drop forging team)

714.55 Forging assistant (power hammer team)
714.60 Forging assistant (heavy press team)
714.65 Smith's striker
714.70 Forging machine operator
714.75 Bending press operator (hot work)
714.98 Trainee
714.99 Other forging occupations

715 Metal Plating and Coating Occupations
715.05 Electroplater (hand)
715.10 Electroformer
715.15 Operator (electrolytic tinning line) (steel strip)
715.20 Tinner (hot dip)
715.25 Hot dip operator (continuous tinning plant)
715.30 Flame plating equipment operator
715.35 Mirror silverer (excluding vacuum metallisation)
715.50 Optical silverer (excluding vacuum metallisation)
715.55 Vacuum metallisation plant operator
715.60 Hot dip assistant (continuous tinning plant)
715.65 Galvanizer (hot dip)
715.70 Galvanizer (continuous electrolytic plant)
715.75 Electrolytic tinning line assistant
715.80 Electroplating machine operator
715.85 Metal sprayer
715.98 Trainee
715.99 Other metal plating and coating occupations

716 Metal Annealing and Tempering Occupations
716.10 Heat treatment operator (general)
716.20 Annealer
716.30 Hardener
716.40 Temperer
716.50 Case hardener
716.98 Trainee
716.99 Other metal annealing and tempering occupations

719 Metal Processing, Forming and Treating Occupations Not Elsewhere Classified
719.10 Continuous cleaning plant operator
719.50 Ladleman
719.60 Hot press operator (sintered components)
719.80 Cold press operator (sintered components)
719.81 Sinter plant worker (metal processing)
719.82 Continuous cleaning plant assistant
719.83 Pickler (excluding continuous cleaning plant)
719.84 Labourer (blast furnace)
719.85 Labourer (steel, non-ferrous metal manufacture)
719.86 Rolling mill labourer
719.87 Production helper (metal tube manufacture)

719.88 Foundry labourer
719.89 Labourer (galvanising, tinning)
719.98 Trainee
719.99 Other metal processing, forming and treating occupations not elsewhere classified

72 Machining and Related Occupations (Engineering and Metal Goods Making)

720 Foremen (Machining and Related Occupations (Engineering and Metal Goods Making))
720.10 Foreman (machine shop)
720.20 Foreman (press shop)
720.30 Foreman (automatic machine attendants) (metal working)
720.40 Foreman (fettlers, grinders (excluding machine tool) and polishers)
720.98 Trainee
720.99 Other foremen (machining and related occupations (engineering and metal goods making))

721 Press, Machine Tool and Other Metal Working Machine Setters
721.10 Machine tool setter (excluding electrochemical machine tools)
721.20 Electrochemical machine tool setter
721.30 Press tool setter
721.40 Tool presetter
721.50 Tackler (wire weaving)
721.98 Trainee
721.99 Other press, machine tool and metal working machine setters

722 Machine Tool Setter-Operators (Metal Working)
722.02 Machine tool setter-operator (general)
722.04 Centre lathe turner
722.06 Setter-operator (capstan, turret lathe)
722.08 Roll turner
722.10 Drilling machine setter-operator
722.12 Boring machine setter-operator
722.14 Jig borer
722.16 Milling machine setter-operator
722.18 Grinding machine setter-operator
722.20 Roll grinder
722.22 Setter-operator (lapping, honing machine)
722.24 Planing machine setter-operator
722.26 Setter-operator (shaping, slotting, broaching machine)
722.28 Gear cutting machine setter-operator
722.30 Die-sinking machine setter-operator
722.32 Spark erosion machine setter-operator
722.34 Metal spinner, Flow turning machine operator
722.36 Numerically controlled machine tool operator
722.38 Driller (circle, faller, hackle)

722.98 Trainee
722.99 Other machine tool setter-operators (metal working)

723 Machine Tool Operators (Metal Working)

723.10 Machine tool operator (general)
723.20 Machine operator (shaping, slotting, broaching machine)
723.50 Semi-automatic lathe operator
723.52 Drilling machine operator
723.54 Boring machine operator
723.56 Milling machine operator
723.58 Grinding machine operator
723.60 Lapping machine operator, Honing machine operator
723.62 Planing machine operator
723.64 Electrochemical machine operator
723.98 Trainee
723.99 Other machine tool operators (metal working)

724 Press and Stamping Machine Operators (Metal Working)

724.10 Flat spring maker
724.50 Hand press operator, Power press operator
724.98 Trainee
724.99 Other press and stamping machine operators (metal working)

725 Automatic Machine Attendants (Metal Working)

725.10 Automatic metal working machine attendant
725.98 Trainee
725.99 Other automatic machine attendants (metal working)

726 Fettling, Grinding (Excluding Machine Tool) and Polishing Occupations (Metal)

726.05 Hand grinder
726.10 Card grinder (textile machinery)
726.15 Mill setter-out (sawmilling)
726.20 Metal polisher (general)
726.25 Lithographic plate preparer
726.50 Metal polisher (specialised)
726.55 Die polisher
726.60 Barrel polishing machine operator
726.65 Chipper (steel dressing), Grinder (steel dressing)
726.90 Fettler
726.92 Shot blaster
726.98 Trainee
726.99 Other fettling, grinding (excluding machine tool) and polishing occupations (metal)

729 Machining and Related Occupations (Engineering and Metal Goods Making) Not Elsewhere Classified

729.02 Chain making machine setter-operator (small links)
729.04 Metal working machine operator
729.06 Tip and die cutter (cemented carbide goods)
729.08 File cutter
729.10 Closing machine operator (wire ropes), Laying up machine operator (wire cable)
729.12 Wire heald maker
729.14 Coiled spring maker
729.16 Tube bender
729.18 Frame bender (ship construction)
729.20 Bending machine operator (sheet metal), Rolling machine operator (sheet metal)
729.22 Router and mounter (process engraving)
729.50 Strander (wire rope, cable)
729.55 Metal straightener (metal stock)
729.60 Beamer (wire weaving)
729.65 Wire finishing machinist
729.70 Twisted-in wire brush maker
729.75 Pen nib maker (general)
729.80 Continuous cut-up line operator
729.90 Continuous cut-up line assistant
729.91 Metal cutting machine operator (excluding continuous cut-up lines)
729.92 Bevelling machinist (tubes, plates)
729.93 Frame bender's helper (ship construction)
729.94 Garment pattern grader (machine)
729.98 Trainee
729.99 Other machining and related occupations (engineering and metal goods making) not elsewhere classified

73 Production Fitting (Metal) and Related Occupations

730 Foremen (Production Fitting (Metal) and Related Occupations)

730.10 Foreman (tool makers, tool fitters and markers-out)
730.20 Foreman (precision instrument making occupations)
730.30 Foreman fitter-assembler (engines)
730.40 Foreman fitter-assembler (machine tools)
730.50 Foreman fitter-assembler (other machinery)
730.98 Trainee
730.99 Other foremen (production fitting (metal) and related occupations)

731 Tool Makers, Tool Fitters and Markers-Out

731.05 Engineering marker-out
731.10 Tool maker (hand and machine)
731.15 Tool maker (hand)
731.20 Press tool maker
731.25 Template maker
731.30 Forme maker
731.35 Tool fitter
731.40 Press tool fitter
731.98 Trainee
731.99 Other tool makers, tool fitters and markers-out

732 Precision Instrument Making Occupations

732.05 Precision instrument maker (excluding optical instruments

732.10 Optical instrument maker

732.15 Watch maker, Clock maker

732.20 Precision instrument fitter (excluding optical instruments)

732.25 Optical instrument fitter

732.98 Trainee

732.99 Other precision instrument making occupations

733 Other Engineering Production Fitters (Excluding Electrical)

733.05 Engineering fitter-assembler (general)

733.10 Engineering fitter-assembler (prototype, experimental)

733.15 Engineering fitter-assembler (aircraft engines)

733.20 Engineering fitter-assembler (marine engines)

733.25 Engineering fitter-assembler (agricultural machinery)

733.30 Engineering fitter-assembler (machine tools)

733.35 Engineering fitter-assembler (other engines and machinery)

733.40 Engineering fitter-assembler (excluding engines and machinery)

733.45 Engineering detail fitter

733.50 Engineering fitter-machinist

733.55 Systems fitter (aircraft)

733.60 Engine tester-rectifier (internal-combustion engines)

733.65 Engine tester-rectifier (jet engine)

733.98 Trainee

733.99 Other engineering production fitters (excluding electrical) not elsewhere classified

734 Other Metal Working Production Fitters

734.05 Metal working fitter-assembler (general)

734.10 Metal working fitter-assembler (motor vehicles)

734.15 Metal working fitter-assembler (machinery)

734.20 Metal working fitter-assembler (excluding motor vehicles and machinery)

734.25 Metal working detail fitter

734.30 Metal working fitter-machinist

734.35 Orthopaedic appliance maker (specialised) (metal)

734.40 Road tester (new motor vehicles)

734.98 Trainee

734.99 Other metal working production fitters not elsewhere classified

739 Production Fitting (Metal) and Related Occupations Not Elsewhere Classified

739.05 Bench hand (engineering)

739.10 Saw maker (circular saws, band-saws)

739.50 Constructional ironworks labourer

739.98 Trainee

739.99 Other production fitting (metal) and related occupations not elsewhere classified

74 Installing, Maintaining and Repairing Occupations (Machines, Instruments and Related Mechanical Equipment)

740 Foremen (Installing, Maintaining and Repairing Occupations (Machines, Instruments and Related Mechanical Equipment))

740.10 Foreman (installation and maintenance fitters and fitter-mechanics (plant, industrial engines and machinery and other mechanical equipment))

740.20 Foreman (fitter-mechanics (motor vehicles))

740.30 Foreman (maintenance fitters and fitter-mechanics (aircraft engines))

740.40 Foreman (precision instrument maintaining and repairing occupations)

740.50 Foreman (office machinery mechanics)

740.98 Trainee

740.99 Other foremen (installing, maintaining and repairing occupations (machines, instruments and related mechanical equipment))

741 Installation and Maintenance Fitters and Fitter-Mechanics (Plant, Industrial Engines and Machinery and Other Mechanical Equipment)

741.02 Machinery erector (mechanical) (installation)

741.04 Aircraft engine installation fitter

741.06 Marine installation fitter

741.08 Maintenance fitter (mechanical) (general)

741.10 Maintenance fitter (civil engineering plant and machinery)

741.12 Maintenance fitter (mechanical) (locomotives)

741.14 Maintenance fitter (railway carriages, railway wagons)

741.16 Maintenance fitter (air-frame)

741.18 Maintenance fitter (other plant and industrial engines and machinery)

741.20 Service fitter (mechanical) (locomotives)

741.22 Service fitter (air-frame)

741.24 Setter fitter-mechanic (textile machinery excluding knitting machines)

741.26 Setter fitter-mechanic (industrial knitting machines)

741.28 Setter fitter-mechanic (other industrial machinery)

741.30 Fitter-mechanic (locks)

741.32 Fitter-mechanic (weighing machines)

741.34 Fitter-mechanic (coin-operated machines excluding weighing machines)

741.36 Mechanic (domestic sewing, knitting machines)

741.38 Cycle mechanic

741.50 Gas appliance mechanic

741.60 Oil burner mechanic

741.70 Jobber (waste preparing machinery)

741.98 Trainee

741.99 Other installation and maintenance fitters and fitter-mechanics (plant, industrial engines and machinery and other mechanical equipment)

742 Fitter-Mechanics (Motor Vehicles)

742.10 Reception mechanic, Road tester (used motor vehicles)

742.20 Motor mechanic

742.30 Motor cycle mechanic

742.98 Trainee

742.99 Other fitter-mechanics (motor vehicles)

743 Maintenance Fitters and Fitter-Mechanics (Aircraft Engines)

743.10 Maintenance fitter (aircraft engine) (general)

743.20 Maintenance fitter (aircraft engine) (specialised)

743.30 Service fitter (aircraft engine)

743.98 Trainee

743.99 Other maintenance fitters and fitter-mechanics (aircraft engines)

744 Precision Instrument Maintaining and Repairing Occupations

744.10 Optical instrument mechanic

744.20 Precision instrument mechanic (excluding optical instruments)

744.30 Watch and clock repairer

744.40 Compass adjuster (marine)

744.98 Trainee

744.99 Other precision instrument maintaining and repairing occupations

745 Office Machinery Maintaining and Repairing Occupations (Mechanical)

745.10 Office machinery mechanic (general)

745.20 Office machinery mechanic (mechanical adding, accounting, calculating machines)

745.30 Typewriter mechanic

745.40 Mechanic (cash till, cash register)

745.98 Trainee

745.99 Other office machinery maintaining and repairing occupations (mechanical)

746 Servicing, Oiling, Greasing and Related Occupations (Mechanical)

746.10 Motor vehicle service man

746.50 Oiler and greaser

746.55 Oiler and bander

746.60 Woollen fettler

746.65 Rollerman (rope haulage)

746.98 Trainee

746.99 Other servicing, oiling, greasing and related occupations (mechanical)

749 Installing, Maintaining and Repairing Occupations (Machines, Instruments and Related Mechanical Equipment) Not Elsewhere Classified

749.05 Service fitter (aircraft engine and air-frame)

749.10 Saw repairer and sharpener

749.15 Shaftsman

749.20 Card nailer

749.25 Stripper and grinder (textile machinery)

749.30 Pin setter (textile machinery)

749.50 Heald mender

749.55 Tyre fitter

749.60 Powered supports maintenance man

749.65 Cleaner (boiler, pipe)

749.70 Conveyor mover

749.98 Trainee

749.99 Other installing, maintaining and repairing occupations (machines, instruments and related mechanical equipment) not elsewhere classified

75 Production Fitting and Wiring Occupations (Electrical and Electronic)

750 Foremen (Production Fitting and Wiring Occupations (Electrical and Electronic))

750.10 Foreman fitter (electrical) (production)

750.20 Foreman fitter (electronics) (production)

750.30 Foreman electrician (production)

750.98 Trainee

750.99 Other foremen (production fitting and wiring occupations (electrical and electronic))

751 Production Fitters (Electrical and Electronic)

751.05 Electrical fitter (general)

751.10 Electrical fitter (prototype, experimental)

751.15 Electrical fitter (switchgear, control equipment)

751.20 Electrical fitter (switchboards)

751.25 Electrical fitter (transformers)

751.30 Electrical fitter (motors, generators, alternators)

751.35 Electrical fitter (other equipment)

751.40 Electronics fitter (general)

751.45 Electronics fitter (prototype, experimental)

751.50 Electronics fitter (telecommunication equipment)

751.55 Electronics fitter (computer equipment)

751.60 Electronics fitter (medical equipment)
751.65 Electronics fitter (other equipment)
751.98 Trainee
751.99 Other production fitters (electrical and electronic)

752 Electricians (Production)

752.10 Aircraft electrician
752.20 Vehicle electrician
752.30 Electrical wireman
752.98 Trainee
752.99 Other electricians (production)

759 Production Fitting and Wiring Occupations (Electrical and Electronic) Not Elsewhere Classified

759.05 Electronics wireman (general)
759.10 Electronics wireman (prototype, experimental)
759.15 Electronics wireman (specialised equipment excluding prototype or experimental)
759.20 Armature winder
759.50 Coil winder (heavy)
759.55 Coil former
759.60 Coil winder (light)
759.65 Cable former
759.98 Trainee
759.99 Other production fitting and wiring occupations (electrical and electronic) not elsewhere classified

76 Installing, Maintaining and Repairing Occupations (Electrical and Electronic)

760 Foremen (Installing, Maintaining and Repairing Occupations (Electrical and Electronic))

760.10 Foreman installation electrician (plant, machinery and other equipment)
760.20 Foreman electrician (maintenance and repair) (plant, machinery and other equipment)
760.30 Foreman electrician (installation, maintenance and repair) (premises and ships)
760.40 Foreman installation fitter (electronic and related equipment)
760.50 Foreman fitter (maintenance and repair) (electronic and related equipment)
760.60 Foreman (linesmen and cable jointers)
760.98 Trainee
760.99 Other foremen (installing, maintaining and repairing occupations (electrical and electronic))

761 Electricians (Installation, Maintenance and Repair) (Plant, Machinery and other Equipment)

761.10 Installation electrician (plant, machinery)
761.20 Maintenance electrician (general) (plant, machinery)
761.30 Maintenance electrician (specialised) (plant, machinery)
761.40 Maintenance electrician (aircraft)
761.50 Service electrician (aircraft)
761.60 Maintenance electrician (motor vehicle)
761.70 Service mechanic (domestic electrical appliances)
761.80 Service mechanic (office electrical machines)
761.98 Trainee
761.99 Other electricians (installation, maintenance and repair) (plant, machinery and other equipment)

762 Electricians (Installation, Maintenance and Repair) (Premises and Ships)

762.10 Electrician (installation and maintenance) (premises)
762.20 Electrician (ship)
762.30 Electrician (theatre, film, television studio)
762.40 Electrical marker-off
762.98 Trainee
762.99 Other electricians (installation, maintenance and repair) (premises and ships)

763 Installing, Maintaining and Repairing Occupations (Electronic and Related Equipment)

763.05 Installer (electronic and related equipment)
763.10 Telephone fitter
763.15 Maintenance fitter (electronic and related equipment) (general)
763.20 Maintenance fitter (aircraft electronic and related equipment)
763.25 Service fitter (aircraft electronic and related equipment)
763.30 Service mechanic (airport electronic and related ground control equipment)
763.35 Maintenance fitter (electronic) (computer equipment)
763.40 Service mechanic (electronic office equipment)
763.45 Service mechanic (electronic test equipment)
763.50 Maintenance fitter (railway signalling and telecommunications equipment)
763.55 Maintenance fitter (sound and television transmission equipment)
763.60 Service mechanic (radar equipment)
763.65 Service mechanic (workshop) (domestic radio, television receivers)
763.70 Service mechanic (field) (domestic radio, television receivers)
763.75 Maintenance fitter (other electronic or related equipment)
763.98 Trainee
763.99 Other installing, maintaining and repairing occupations (electronic and related equipment)

764 Linesmen and Cable Jointers

764.10 Overhead linesman (electricity supply, electric traction)
764.20 Overhead linesman (telecommunications services)
764.30 Cable jointer
764.40 Cable tester (installation)
764.98 Trainee
764.99 Other linesmen and cable jointers

769 Installing, Maintaining and Repairing Occupations (Electrical and Electronic) Not Elsewhere Classified

769.10 Television aerial erector (domestic receivers)
769.20 Meter fixer
769.30 Electrical craftsman's labourer, Electronic craftsman's labourer
769.98 Trainee
769.99 Other installing, maintaining and repairing occupations (electrical and electronic) not elsewhere classified

77 Pipe, Sheet and Structural Metal Working and Related Occupations

770 Foremen (Pipe, Sheet and Structural Metal Working and Related Occupations)

770.10 Foreman (plumbing, heating and ventilating and pipe fitting occupations)
770.20 Foreman (sheet metal working occupations)
770.30 Foreman (metal plate working and riveting occupations)
770.40 Foreman (steel erecting and rigging and cable splicing occupations)
770.50 Foreman (welding and flame cutting occupations)
770.98 Trainee
770.99 Other foremen (pipe, sheet and structural metal working and related occupations)

771 Plumbing, Heating and Ventilating and Pipe Fitting Occupations

771.05 Plumber (construction)
771.10 Ship plumber
771.15 Chemical plumber
771.20 Gas fitter
771.25 Heating and ventilating engineering fitter
771.30 Pipe fitter (fabrication)
771.35 Pipe fitter (installation, maintenance)
771.40 Ductwork erector
771.98 Trainee
771.99 Other plumbing, heating and ventilating and pipe fitting occupations

772 Sheet Metal Working Occupations

772.05 Marker-out
772.10 Sheet metal worker
772.15 Coppersmith
772.20 Panel beater (vehicle body repair)
772.25 Panel beater (excluding vehicle body repair)
772.30 Engine radiator repairer
772.35 Stencil plate maker (hand)
772.40 Metal pattern maker (footwear)
772.98 Trainee
772.99 Other sheet metal working occupations

773 Metal Plate Working and Riveting Occupations

773.02 Marker-off (metal plate, structural metal)
773.04 Plater (unspecified)
773.06 Ship's plater
773.08 Boiler plater
773.10 Constructional plater
773.12 Shipwright (metal)
773.14 Driller (constructional metal work)
773.16 Riveter
773.18 Caulker
773.20 Steelworker (general) (ship construction, repair)
773.50 Holder-up
773.98 Trainee
773.99 Other metal plate working and riveting occupations

774 Steel Erecting and Rigging and Cable Splicing Occupations

774.05 Rigger (engineering plant and machinery)
774.10 Rigger (dock)
774.15 Rigger (ship)
774.20 Steel erector
774.25 Scaffolder (metal scaffolding)
774.30 Stager (shipbuilding and repairing)
774.35 Splicer (wire rope) (general)
774.50 Steel bender and fixer
774.55 Ropeman
774.60 Splicer (wire rope) (specialised)
774.90 Metal shuttering erector
774.98 Trainee
774.99 Other steel erecting and rigging and cable splicing occupations

775 Welding and Flame Cutting Occupations (Metal)

775.05 Welder (general)
775.10 Gas welder
775.15 Electric arc welder
775.20 Electron beam welder
775.25 Thermit welder
775.30 Hand burner
775.35 Flame dresser (rolling mills)
775.50 Machine burner
775.90 Welding machine operator (non-repetitive)
775.92 Brazer, Solderer (non-repetitive)
775.98 Trainee
775.99 Other welding and flame cutting occupations (metal)

776 Pipe, Sheet and Structural Metal Workers' Mates and Labourers

776.10 Mate (plumber's, pipe fitter's, heating and ventilating engineering fitter's)
776.20 Gas fitter's mate
776.30 Plater's helper
776.40 Shipwright's labourer
776.50 Steel erector's mate
776.60 Rigger's labourer (ship)
776.70 Steelworker's labourer (ship construction, repair)
776.99 Other pipe, sheet and structural metal worker's mates and labourers

779 Pipe, Sheet and Structural Metal Working and Related Occupations Not Elsewhere Classified

779.10 Ornamental metal worker
779.50 Rivet heater
779.98 Trainee
779.99 Other pipe, sheet and structural metal working and related occupations not elsewhere classified

79 Processing, Making, Repairing and Related Occupations (Metal and Electrical) Not Elsewhere Classified

790 Foremen (Processing, Making, Repairing and Related Occupations (Metal and Electrical) Not Elsewhere Classified)

790.10 Foreman (goldsmiths, silversmiths, precious stone working and related occupations)
790.20 Foreman (metal engraving occupations)
790.30 Foreman (vehicle body builders, aircraft finishers)
790.98 Trainee
790.99 Other foremen (processing, making, repairing and related occupations (metal and electrical) not elsewhere classified)

791 Goldsmiths, Silversmiths, Precious Stone Working and Related Occupations

791.02 Goldsmith, Silversmith
791.04 Britannia metal smith
791.06 Chaser
791.08 Saw piercer
791.10 Engine turner
791.12 Chain maker (hand) (gold, silver)
791.14 Goldbeater
791.16 Cutter and booker (metal leaf)
791.18 Diamond sawyer, Diamond cleaver
791.20 Diamond cutter, Diamond polisher
791.22 Gem cutter and polisher (excluding diamonds)
791.24 Jewellery model maker
791.26 Jeweller (general)
791.28 Jobbing jeweller
791.30 Jewellery mounter
791.32 Gem setter
791.34 Industrial diamond setter

791.98 Trainee
791.99 Other goldsmiths, silversmiths, precious stone working and related occupations

792 Metal Engraving Occupations

792.02 Roller engraver (hand)
792.04 Printing plate engraver (hand)
792.06 Roller engraver (pantograph machine), Printing plate engraver (pantograph machine)
792.08 Clammer (roller engraving)
792.10 Roller engraver (mill engraving machine)
792.12 Die engraver
792.14 Etcher
792.16 Electronic engraver (process engraving)
792.18 Decorative engraver (hand)
792.20 Pantograph engraving machine setter-operator (excluding printing plates and rollers)
792.50 Pantograph engraving machine operator (excluding printing rollers and plates)
792.98 Trainee
792.99 Other metal engraving occupations

793 Vehicle Body Builders and Aircraft Finishers

793.10 Vehicle body builder
793.20 Vehicle body finisher
793.30 Aircraft finisher
793.98 Trainee
793.99 Other vehicle body builders and aircraft finishers

799 Other Processing, Making, Repairing and Related Occupations (Metal and Electrical)

799.02 Installation fitter (electrical and mechanical)
799.04 Maintenance fitter (electrical and mechanical)
799.06 Metal working and woodworking machines setter-operator
799.08 Wireworker (bench hand)
799.10 Barrel setter
799.12 Motor cycle rectifier
799.14 Saw smith
799.16 Design cutter (printing rollers, blocks)
799.18 Marker maker (footwear)
799.20 Card setting machine tenter
799.50 Card fillet dresser
799.52 Card top clipper
799.54 Filler-up (card clothing)
799.56 Needle straightener
799.58 Cycle frame setter
799.60 Cycle wheel truer
799.62 Measurer, coiler and cutter (wire rope, wire cable)
799.90 Fitter's mate
799.98 Trainee
799.99 Other processing, making, repairing and related occupations (metal and electrical) not elsewhere classified

Major Group XV PAINTING, REPETITIVE ASSEMBLING, PRODUCT INSPECTING, PACKAGING AND RELATED OCCUPATIONS

81 Painting and Related Coating Occupations

810 Foremen (Painting and Related Occupations)

810.10 Foreman (painting and decorating occupations) (structures)
810.20 Foreman (painting and related coating occupations) (brush) (excluding structures)
810.30 Foreman (painting and related coating occupations) (spray) (excluding structures)
810.40 Foreman (painting and related coating occupations) (dip)
810.50 Foreman (wood staining, waxing and French polishing occupations) (hand)
810.98 Trainee
810.99 Other foremen (painting and related coating occupations)

811 Painting and Decorating Occupations (Structures)

811.10 Painter and decorator
811.20 Painter (buildings), Ship painter
811.30 Paperhanger
811.50 Painter (metal structures), Red leader
811.98 Trainee
811.99 Other painting and decorating occupations (structures)

812 Painting and Related Coating Occupations (Brush) (Excluding Structures)

812.05 Signwriter, Show-card writer
812.10 Glass painter
812.15 Ceramics painter (freehand)
812.20 Ceramics enameller
812.25 Ceramics toucher-up (decorating)
812.50 Ceramics bander, Ceramics liner
812.60 Ceramics coater
812.70 Painter (excluding ceramics, glass)
812.90 Slip painting machine attendant
812.98 Trainee
812.99 Other painting and related coating occupations (brush) (excluding structures)

813 Painting and Related Coating Occupations (Spray) (Excluding Structures)

813.10 Spray polisher (wood) (hand)
813.20 Spray painter (aircraft, vehicles) (hand)
813.50 Spray glazer (hand), Spray painter (ceramics) (hand)
813.55 Spray painter (not elsewhere classified) (hand)
813.60 Electrostatic paint sprayer (hand), Electrostatic polish sprayer (hand)
813.65 Spray painting machine operator
813.70 Electrostatic spray painting plant operator, Electrostatic spray polishing plant operator
813.75 Spray dyer (hand)
813.90 Glaze spraying machine attendant, Spray painting machine attendant (ceramics)
813.92 Spray painting machine attendant (excluding ceramics)
813.98 Trainee
813.99 Other painting and related coating occupations (spray) (excluding structures)

814 Painting and Related Coating Occupations (Dip)

814.10 Ceramics dipper (hand)
814.20 Dipper (excluding ceramics) (hand)
814.30 Electrophoretic painting plant operator
814.50 Dip painting machine attendant
814.98 Trainee
814.99 Other painting and related coating occupations (dip)

815 Wood Staining, Waxing and French Polishing Occupations (Hand)

815.10 French polisher
815.98 Trainee
815.99 Other wood staining, waxing and French polishing occupations (hand)

819 Painting and Related Coating Occupations Not Elsewhere Classified

819.05 Glass decorator (general)
819.10 Groundlayer
819.15 Ceramics stenciller
819.20 Coach painter
819.25 Wallpaper grounder
819.30 Jewellery enameller
819.50 Sponge mottler
819.55 Ceramics lithographer, Painter's transferrer (ceramics)
819.60 Toucher-up (glaze)
819.65 Curtain-coating machine operator (excluding ceramics)
819.70 Polisher's filler-in
819.90 Tube liner
819.91 Curtain-glazing machine attendant
819.92 Painting machine attendant (ceramics) (pad, roller)
819.93 Curtain-coating machine attendant (excluding ceramics), Flow-coating machine attendant (excluding ceramics)
819.94 Flatter
819.95 Polisher finisher
819.98 Trainee
819.99 Other painting and related coating occupations not elsewhere classified

82 Product Assembling Occupations (Repetitive)

820 Foremen (Product Assembling Occupations (Repetitive))
820.10 Foreman (product assembling occupations (repetitive))
820.98 Trainee

821 Product Assembling Occupations (Repetitive)
821.05 Repetitive assembler (mineral products)
821.10 Repetitive assembler (paper, paperboard products)
821.15 Repetitive assembler (textile products)
821.20 Repetitive assembler (leather goods)
821.25 Repetitive assembler (wood products)
821.30 Repetitive assembler (rubber, plastics goods)
821.35 Repetitive assembler (metal goods) (hand)
821.40 Repetitive assembler (metal goods) (machine)
821.45 Repetitive assembler (electrical, electronic goods)
821.99 Other product assembling occupations (repetitive)

83 Product Inspecting, Examining, Sorting, Grading and Measuring Occupations (Excluding Laboratory Technicians)

830 Foremen (Product Inspecting, Examining, Sorting, Grading and Measuring Occupations (Excluding Laboratory Technicians))
830.10 Foreman (inspecting and testing occupations) (metal and electrical engineering)
830.20 Foreman (examining, viewing and checking occupations) (metal and electrical engineering)
830.30 Foreman (examining, viewing and checking occupations) (excluding metal and electrical engineering)
830.40 Foreman (sorting and grading occupations)
830.98 Trainee
830.99 Other foremen (product inspecting, examining, sorting, grading and measuring occupations (excluding laboratory technicians))

831 Inspecting and Testing Occupations (Metal and Electrical Engineering)
831.05 Inspector (metal castings)
831.10 Inspector (forgings)
831.15 Inspector (tool room)
831.20 Inspector (aircraft assembly)
831.25 Inspector (metal) (not elsewhere classified)
831.30 Electrical inspector (aircraft)
831.35 Engine tester (internal-combustion engine)
831.40 Engine tester (jet engine)
831.45 Tester (electrical plant and industrial machinery)
831.50 Systems tester (electronics)
831.55 Test welder
831.98 Trainee
831.99 Other inspecting and testing occupations (metal and electrical engineering)

382 Examining, Viewing and Checking Occupations (Metal and Electrical Engineering)
832.10 Examiner (vehicle body)
832.50 Examiner (metal, metal products) (not elsewhere classified)
832.55 Examiner (electrical, electronic equipment)
832.60 Checking equipment operator (metal)
832.65 Checker (electrical, electronic equipment)
832.98 Trainee
832.99 Other examining, viewing and checking occupations (metal and electrical engineering)

833 Examining, Viewing and Checking Occupations (Excluding Metal and Electrical Engineering)
833.05 Examiner (yarn)
833.10 Examiner (textile fabric)
833.15 Examiner (tobacco, tobacco products)
833.20 Examiner (wood, wood products)
833.25 Examiner (paper, paperboard)
833.30 Examiner (mineral products)
833.35 Examiner (garments, textile products)
833.40 Examiner (leather products)
833.45 Examiner (plastics, rubber)
833.50 Examiner (materials, products) (not elsewhere classified)
833.55 Checking equipment operator (excluding metal and electrical and electronic equipment)
833.90 Examiner (food products)
833.98 Trainee
833.99 Other examining, viewing and check-occupations (excluding metal and electrical engineering)

834 Sorting and Grading Occupations
834.05 Grader-sorter (hides, skins, leather)
834.10 Grader-sorter (pelts)
834.15 Grader (raw wool)
834.20 Grader (metal production)
834.25 Scrap metal sorter
834.50 Rag sorter

834.55 Grader (textile fabric, textile products)
834.60 Grader (tobacco pipe)
834.65 Grader-sorter (fish)
834.70 Grader (ceramics)
834.90 Fibre sorter
834.92 Sorter (laundering, dry cleaning, dyeing)
834.94 Sorter (hand) (materials, products) (not elsewhere classified)
834.98 Trainee
834.99 Other sorting and grading occupations

835 Weighing and Measuring Occupations

835.10 Weigher (production)
835.20 Weigher (goods, products)
835.30 Weigher (weighbridge)
835.40 Measuring machine operator (linear)
835.50 Measuring machine operator (area)
835.98 Trainee
835.99 Other weighing and measuring occupations

839 Product Inspecting, Examining, Sorting, Grading and Measuring Occupations (Excluding Laboratory Technicians) Not Elsewhere Classified

839.10 Examiner (optical elements)
839.20 Prescription checker (ophthalmic)
839.30 Tester (chemical, chemical and physical) (routine)
839.50 Goods vehicle tester
839.90 Examiner (laundering, cleaning, dyeing)
839.98 Trainee
839.99 Other product inspecting, examining, sorting, grading and measuring occupations (excluding laboratory technicians) not elsewhere classified

84 Packaging, Labelling and Related Occupations

840 Foremen (Packaging, Labelling and Related Occupations)

840.10 Foreman (packaging, labelling and related occupations)
840.98 Trainee

841 Packaging, Labelling and Related Occupations (Hand)

841.05 Gas cylinder filler
841.10 Packer (heavy goods)
841.15 Packer (chemical, pharmaceutical and allied products)
841.20 Packer (food, horticultural products)
841.25 Packer (glass, china)
841.30 Packer (laundry, dry cleaning, dyeing)
841.35 Packer (textiles)
841.40 Packer (other goods)
841.50 Folder (textiles)
841.60 Labeller
841.98 Trainee
841.99 Other hand packaging, labelling and related occupations

842 Packaging, Labelling and Related Occupations (Machine)

842.10 Container filler (excluding bottles, jars and cans)
842.20 Wrapping machine attendant
842.30 Bottling machine attendant
842.40 Canning machine attendant (food, drink)
842.50 Canning machine attendant (excluding food and drink)
842.60 Labelling machine attendant
842.98 Trainee
842.99 Other packaging, labelling and related occupations (machine)

Major Group XVI CONSTRUCTION, MINING AND RELATED OCCUPATIONS NOT ELSEWHERE CLASSIFIED

86 Construction and Related Occupations Not Elsewhere Classified

860 Foremen (Construction and Related Occupations Not Elsewhere Classified)

860.05 Foreman bricklayer
860.10 Foreman fixer mason
860.15 Foreman plasterer
860.20 Foreman (terrazzo working, tile setting occupations)
860.25 Foreman (roofing occupations)
860.30 Foreman glazier
860.35 Foreman (road making and repairing occupations) (excluding machine operating)
860.40 Foreman (trackmen and platelayers)
860.45 Area works inspector (railway)
860.50 Permanent way inspector (railway)
860.55 Foreman (concrete erecting occupations)
860.98 Trainee
860.99 Other foremen (construction and related occupations not elsewhere classified)

861 Bricklaying and Stone Setting Occupations

861.10 Bricklayer (construction)
861.20 Refractory bricklayer
861.30 Bricklayer (industrial chimneys)
861.40 Fixer mason
861.50 Trowel worker (general)
861.98 Trainee
861.99 Other bricklaying and stone setting occupations

862 Plastering Occupations

862.10 Plasterer (solid work)
862.20 Plasterer (fibrous work)

862 .98 Trainee
862 .99 Other plastering occupations

863 Terrazzo Working and Tile Setting Occupations

863 .10 Terrazzo layer
863 .20 Granolithic layer
863 .30 Floor and wall tiler
863 .40 Mosaic design layer
863 .50 Fireplace builder
863 .60 Terrazzo polisher (hand)
863 .70 Terrazzo polisher (machine)
863 .98 Trainee
863 .99 Other terrazzo working and tile setting occupations

864 Roofing Occupations

864 .10 Roof slater and tiler
864 .20 Thatcher
864 .30 Roofing felt fixer
864 .40 Sheet fixer (roofs, exterior walls)
864 .98 Trainee
864 .99 Other roofing occupations

865 Glazing Occupations

865 .10 Glazier
865 .20 Patent roofing glazier
865 .30 Screen glazier (vehicles)
865 .40 Leaded light maker
865 .98 Trainee
865 .99 Other glazing occupations

866 Road and Railway Track Making and Repairing Occupations (Excluding Machine Operating)

866 .10 Pavior and kerb layer
866 .20 Trackman
866 .30 Platelayer
866 .50 General roadman
866 .60 Raker (asphalt, bitumen, tar paving)
866 .90 Tamperman (asphalt paving)
866 .92 Road lengthsman
866 .98 Trainee
866 .99 Other road and railway track making and repairing occupations (excluding machine operating)

867 Concrete Erecting Occupations

867 .10 Concrete erector
867 .98 Trainee
867 .99 Other concrete erecting occupations

868 Building and Civil Engineering Craftsmen's Mates and Labourers Not Elsewhere Classified

868 .02 Craftsman's mate (general)
868 .04 Bricklayer's mate
868 .06 Fixer mason's mate
868 .08 Plasterer's mate
868 .10 Terrazzo layer's mate, Granolithic layer's mate
868 .12 Floor and wall tiler's mate
868 .14 Roof slater and tiler's mate
868 .16 Roofing felt fixer's mate
868 .18 Sheet fixer's mate (roofing, walling)

868 .20 Steeplejack's mate
868 .50 Builder's labourer (general)
868 .60 Civil engineering labourer (general)
868 .70 Trenchman
868 .98 Trainee
868 .99 Other building and civil engineering craftsmen's mates and labourers not elsewhere classified

869 Other Construction and Related Occupations

869 .02 Builder (general)
869 .04 Steeplejack
869 .06 Fence erector
869 .08 Mastic asphalt spreader
869 .10 Composition floor layer
869 .12 Linoleum fitter
869 .14 Ceiling fixer
869 .16 Blind fixer
869 .18 Land drainage worker
869 .20 Sewerman
869 .22 Insulator (structures) (hand)
869 .24 Insulator (structures) (machine)
869 .26 Insulator (boilers, pipes, plant, equipment)
869 .28 Pipe layer
869 .30 Pipe jointer
869 .32 Pipe layer and jointer
869 .34 Waste prevention inspector (water supply)
869 .36 Diver, Frogman
869 .50 Timberman (surface excavations)
869 .52 Demolisher
869 .54 Concreter (site work)
869 .56 Installer (auxiliary track equipment)
869 .58 Plasterboard fixer, Dry liner
869 .60 Cleaner (structural stone, brickwork)
869 .62 Restorer (stonework, brickwork)
869 .64 Reservoir attendant
869 .66 Potman
869 .68 Handyman (residential establishments)
869 .70 Diver's linesman
869 .90 Grave digger
869 .98 Trainee
869 .99 Other construction and related occupations not elsewhere classified

87 Mining, Quarrying, Well Drilling and Related Occupations Not Elsewhere Classified

870 Foremen (Mining, Quarrying, Well Drilling and Related Occupations Not Elsewhere Classified)

870 .10 Foreman (drilling and shot firing occupations)
870 .20 Foreman (tunnelling occupations)
870 .30 Deputy (coalmining)
870 .98 Trainee
870 .99 Other foremen (mining, quarrying, well drilling and related occupations not elsewhere classified)

871 Drilling and Shotfiring Occupations

871.05 Driller (coalmining)
871.10 Well drilling operative
871.15 Shotfirer (coalmining)
871.20 Shotfirer (excluding coalmining)
871.50 Driller (excluding coalmining or well drilling)
871.98 Trainee
871.99 Other drilling and shotfiring occupations

872 Tunnelling Occupations

872.10 Ripper (coalmining)
872.20 Tunnel miner (excluding coalmining)
872.98 Trainee
872.99 Other tunnelling occupations

873 Underground Coalmining Occupations Not Elsewhere Classified

873.05 Face console operator (remotely operated longwall face (ROLF) installation)
873.10 Power loader man
873.15 Coal cutting-loading machine operator (longwall face)
873.20 Coal cutting-loading machine assistant (longwall face)
873.25 Coal cutterman
873.30 Coal cutting machine assistant
873.35 Collier
873.40 Packer
873.45 Power stower
873.98 Trainee
873.99 Other underground coalmining occupations not elsewhere classified

879 Other Mining, Quarrying, Well Drilling and Related Occupations

879.10 Miner (excluding coalmining)
879.20 Timberer (mining)
879.30 Wasteman (mining)
879.50 Cutting machine operator (mining excluding coal)
879.90 Tunnel miner's labourer
879.98 Trainee
879.99 Other mining, quarrying, well drilling and related occupations not elsewhere classified

Major Group XVII TRANSPORT OPERATING, MATERIALS MOVING AND STORING AND RELATED OCCUPATIONS

91 Water Transport Operating Occupations

910 Foremen (Water Transport Operating Occupations)

910.10 Boatswain (excluding fishing vessel)
910.20 Donkeyman
910.30 Engine room storekeeper
910.40 Foreman lighterman
910.50 Dock foreman
910.98 Trainee
910.99 Other foremen (water transport operating occupations)

911 Deck and Engine Room Ratings

911.05 Quartermaster
911.10 Seaman
911.15 Boatman
911.20 Senior mechanic
911.50 Engine room rating
911.60 Engineer mechanic (fishing or coastal ship, or craft on inland waters)
911.98 Trainee
911.99 Other deck and engine room rating

919 Water Transport Operating Occupations Not Elsewhere Classified

919.10 Lighthouse keeper
919.20 Survey sounder
919.50 Berthing man
919.60 Bridge man
919.70 Lock gateman (inland waterways and docks)
919.98 Trainee
919.99 Other water transport operating occupations not elsewhere classified

92 Rail Transport Operating Occupations

920 Foremen and Inspectors (Rail Transport Operating Occupations)

920.10 Train crew inspector
920.20 Foreman (marshalling yard)
920.30 Inspector regulator
920.40 Movements inspector
920.98 Trainee
920.99 Other foremen and inspectors (rail transport operating occupations)

921 Drivers and Secondmen (Rail Transport)

921.10 Locomotive driver (standard gauge)
921.20 Secondman (rail)
921.50 Locomotive driver (narrow gauge)
921.60 Locomotive driver (mine)
921.98 Trainee
921.99 Other drivers and secondmen (rail transport)

922 Guards (Rail Transport)

922.10 Conductor guard
922.20 Guard (surface railway)
922.30 Guard (underground railway excluding mine)
922.40 Loco guard (mine)
922.98 Trainee
922.99 Other guards (rail transport)

923 Traffic Controlling Occupations (Rail Transport)

923.10 Head shunter
923.50 Shunter

C01—D

923 .60 Signalman (rail)
923 .98 Trainee
923 .99 Other traffic controlling occupations

93 Road Transport Operating Occupations

930 Foremen and Inspectors (Road Transport Operating Occupations)

930 .10 Inspector (public service vehicles)
930 .20 Depot foreman (motor vehicles)
930 .30 Depot foreman (horse-drawn vehicles)
930 .98 Trainee
930 .99 Other foremen and inspectors (road transport operating occupations)

931 Omnibus and Coach Drivers

931 .10 Omnibus driver, Coach driver
931 .20 Driver (one-man-operated omnibus)
931 .98 Trainee
931 .99 Other omnibus and coach drivers

932 Heavy Goods Vehicle Drivers

932 .10 Heavy goods vehicle driver (excluding articulated vehicle)
932 .20 Articulated vehicle driver
932 .98 Trainee
932 .99 Other heavy goods vehicle drivers

933 Other Motor Vehicle Drivers

933 .10 Light goods vehicle driver
933 .20 Taxi driver
933 .30 Motor car driver
933 .40 Mechanical road sweeper driver
933 .50 Road patrolman
933 .98 Trainee
933 .99 Other motor vehicle drivers

934 Conductors (Road Transport)

934 .10 Conductor (public service vehicle)
934 .98 Trainee

935 Drivers' Mates (Road Transport)

935 .10 Driver's mate
935 .98 Trainee

939 Road Transport Operating Occupations Not Elsewhere Classified

939 .10 Driver (horse-drawn vehicle)
939 .98 Trainee
939 .99 Other road transport operating occupations not elsewhere classified

94 Civil Engineering and Materials Handling Equipment Operating Occupations

940 Foremen (Civil Engineering and Materials Handling Equipment Operating Occupations)

940 .10 Foreman (earth moving and civil engineering equipment operating occupations)
940 .20 Foreman (crane, hoist and other materials handling equipment operating occupations)
940 .98 Trainee
940 .99 Other foremen (civil engineering and materials handling equipment operating occupations)

941 Earth Moving and Civil Engineering Equipment Operating Occupations

941 .10 Pile driver
941 .20 Driver (asphalt spreading machine)
941 .30 Leveller (asphalt spreading machine)
941 .50 Road roller driver
941 .55 Dredger driver
941 .60 Grader driver
941 .65 Mechanical excavator driver
941 .70 Mechanical shovel driver
941 .90 Bulldozer driver
941 .92 Operator (concrete paving machine)
941 .94 Sprayer (tar, bitumen)
941 .98 Trainee
941 .99 Other earth moving and civil engineering equipment operating occupations

942 Crane, Hoist and Other Materials Handling Equipment Operating Occupations

942 .05 Winding engineman (mine)
942 .10 Cageman
942 .15 Bunker control man (underground)
942 .20 Bunker control man (surface)
942 .25 Manipulator driver
942 .30 Straddle carrier driver
942 .50 Jib crane driver
942 .52 Tower crane driver
942 .54 Mobile crane driver
942 .56 Overhead crane driver
942 .58 Hoist driver
942 .60 Winch driver
942 .62 Trolley driver, Lifting truck driver
942 .64 Dumper driver
942 .66 Charger car driver
942 .68 Charger driver (iron and steel)
942 .70 Cupola charger (foundry)
942 .72 Pusherman (coal-gas oven, coke oven)
942 .74 Coke carman (coal-gas oven, coke oven)
942 .76 Crane slinger
942 .78 Loader (bulk materials)
942 .80 Operator (gathering arm loader)
942 .82 Conveyer operator
942 .98 Trainee
942 .99 Other crane, hoist and materials handling equipment operating occupations

949 Civil Engineering and Materials Handling Equipment Operating Occupations Not Elsewhere Classified

949 .10 Aircraft refueller
949 .50 Tanker filler (liquids, gases)
949 .55 Tippler operator
949 .60 Coke guide man (coal-gas oven, coke oven)

949.65 Rope runner
949.98 Trainee
949.99 Other civil engineering and materials handling equipment operating occupations not elsewhere classified

95 Transport Operating, Materials Moving and Storing and Related Occupations Not Elsewhere Classified

950 Foremen (Transport Operating, Materials Moving and Storing and Related Occupations Not Elsewhere Classified)

950.10 Foreman storekeeper
950.20 Foreman (stevedores, dockers and related occupations)
950.98 Trainee
950.99 Other foremen (transport operating, materials moving and storing and related occupations not elsewhere classified)

951 Storekeepers, Warehousemen

951.05 Storekeeper (industrial)
951.10 Warehouseman (furniture depository)
951.15 Baggage master
951.20 Cellarman
951.25 Timber tallyman
951.50 Warehouseman (wholesale, retail distribution)
951.55 Storekeeper (excluding industrial)
951.60 Linen keeper
951.65 Lampman (mining)
951.90 Warehouseman (freight)
951.92 Intakeman (grain, sugar and similar materials)
951.94 Fuel issuer (transport depot)
951.98 Trainee
951.99 Other storekeepers, warehousemen

952 Stevedores, Dockers and Related Occupations

952.10 Docker
952.20 Goods porter (canal)
952.30 Jetty operator (bulk liquids, gases)
952.40 Fish lumper
952.50 Dock waterman
952.98 Trainee
952.99 Other stevedores, dockers and related occupations

959 Other Transport Operating, Materials Moving and Storing and Related Occupations

959.10 Furniture remover
959.50 Porter (warehouse, store, shop, market, slaughterhouse)
959.55 Materials handler (works)
959.60 Aircraft marshaller
959.65 Loader (vehicle, aircraft)
959.70 Baggage porter (docks, air terminal)
959.75 Loader (wagon, mine car or similar container), Tub manipulator
959.80 Kiln unloader (ceramics goods)
959.85 Refuse collector
959.98 Trainee
959.99 Other transport operating, materials moving and storing and related occupations not elsewhere classified

Major Group XVIII MISCELLANEOUS OCCUPATIONS

97 Machinery, Plant and Equipment Operating Occupations Not Elsewhere Classified

970 Foremen (Machinery, Plant and Equipment Operating Occupations Not Elsewhere Classified)

970.10 Foreman (boiler and power generating machinery operating occupations)
970.20 Foreman (valveman, turncocks and related occupations)
970.30 Foreman (electrical switchboard attending occupations)
970.98 Trainee
970.99 Other foremen (machinery, plant and equipment operating occupations not elsewhere classified)

971 Boiler and Power Generating Machinery Operating Occupations

971.05 Plant operator (nuclear generating station)
971.10 Unit operator (power station)
971.15 Boiler operator (steam generating)
971.20 Turbine operator
971.50 Stationary engine driver
971.55 Assistant unit operator (power station)
971.60 Gas compressor operator
971.90 Air compressor operator
971.91 Crematorium furnace attendant
971.92 Boiler operator (hot water supply)
971.93 Incinerator operator
971.98 Trainee
971.99 Other boiler and power generating machinery operating occupations

972 Valvemen, Turncocks and Related Occupations

972.10 Control room operator (gas supply)
972.50 Valveman (materials flow)
972.60 Turncock
972.98 Trainee
972.99 Other valvemen, turncocks and related occupations

973 Electricity Switchboard Attending Occupations

973 .10   Switchboard attendant (electricity supply)
973 .50   Substation attendant (electricity supply)
973 .98   Trainee
973 .99   Other electricity switchboard attending occupations

979 Other Machinery, Plant and Equipment Operating Occupations

979 .10   Auxiliary plant attendant (power generating)
979 .50   Pumpman
979 .55   Cylinder preparer
979 .60   Washing plant attendant (vehicles)
979 .65   Washing machine attendant (containers)
979 .98   Trainee
979 .99   Other machinery, plant and equipment operating occupations not elsewhere classified

99 Miscellaneous Occupations Not Elsewhere Classified

990 Supervisors and Foremen Not Elsewhere Classified

990 .00   Supervisor (unspecified), Foreman (unspecified)
990 .10   Supervisor (miscellaneous occupations not elsewhere classified), Foreman (miscellaneous occupations not elsewhere classified)
990 .20   Supervisor (occupations straddling major groups), Foreman (occupations straddling major groups)
990 .98   Trainee

991 Labourers and General Hands Not Elsewhere Classified

991 .10   Heavy labourer (not elsewhere classified)
991 .20   Light labourer (not elsewhere classified), Factory worker (general) (not elsewhere classified)
991 .30   Stage hand

999 Other Occupations

999 .99   Other occupations not elsewhere classified

LIST OF KEY OCCUPATIONS FOR STATISTICAL PURPOSES

Group titles

GROUP

I   MANAGERIAL (GENERAL MANAGEMENT)

II   PROFESSIONAL AND RELATED SUPPORTING MANAGEMENT AND ADMINISTRATION

III   PROFESSIONAL AND RELATED IN EDUCATION, WELFARE AND HEALTH

IV   LITERARY, ARTISTIC AND SPORTS

V   PROFESSIONAL AND RELATED IN SCIENCE, ENGINEERING, TECHNOLOGY AND SIMILAR FIELDS

VI   MANAGERIAL (EXCLUDING GENERAL MANAGEMENT)

VII   CLERICAL AND RELATED

VIII   SELLING

IX   SECURITY AND PROTECTIVE SERVICE

X   CATERING, CLEANING, HAIRDRESSING AND OTHER PERSONAL SERVICE

XI   FARMING, FISHING AND RELATED

XII   MATERIALS PROCESSING (EXCLUDING METAL)
[hides, textiles, chemicals, food, drink and tobacco, wood, paper and board, rubber and plastics]

XIII   MAKING AND REPAIRING (EXCLUDING METAL AND ELECTRICAL)
[glass, ceramics, printing, paper products, clothing, footwear, woodworking, rubber and plastics]

XIV   PROCESSING, MAKING, REPAIRING AND RELATED (METAL AND ELECTRICAL)
[iron, steel and other metals, engineering (including installation and maintenance) vehicles and shipbuilding]

XV   PAINTING, REPETITIVE ASSEMBLING, PRODUCT INSPECTING, PACKAGING AND RELATED

XVI   CONSTRUCTION, MINING AND RELATED NOT IDENTIFIED ELSEWHERE

XVII   TRANSPORT OPERATING, MATERIALS MOVING AND STORING AND RELATED

XVIII   MISCELLANEOUS

KEY LIST

GROUP I MANAGERIAL (GENERAL MANAGEMENT)

Note: This group covers top level managers, whose work is primarily policy formulation, long-term planning and major decision taking and usually involves multi-functional control

Top managers—national government and other non-trading organisations	001 (All)	002 .65

Notes

1. Includes ministers, MPs, under secretaries and above in the civil service, town managers and equivalent top-management posts in other non-trading organisations

2. Excludes senior staff of universities and hospitals (Group III) and of local authorities except town managers (Groups II, III, V and VI)

General, central, divisional managers—trading organisations	002 (All except 002 .65)

Notes

1. Includes (1) chairmen and managing directors

> *(2) company directors (not elsewhere identified) of firms with 500 or more employees*

2. Excludes (1) principals and partners in professional practice eg architecture, accountancy, dentistry, medicine, law (Groups II, III and V)

> *(2) master craftsmen (Groups X, XIII, XIV, XV and XVI) eg electrical contractor, plumber*

> *(3) farmers and horticulturists (employers and self-employed) (Group VI)*

> *(4) shopkeepers (employers and self-employed) (Group VI)*

GROUP II PROFESSIONAL AND RELATED SUPPORTING MANAGEMENT AND ADMINISTRATION

Judges, barristers, advocates and solicitors	021 (All)	022 (All)
Company secretaries	031 .10	
Town Clerks and other clerks to local authorities	031 .20	
Secretaries of trade associations, trade unions, professional bodies and charities	031 .30 031 .40	031 .50 031 .60
Accountants	032 (All)	
Estimators, valuers and assessors	033 (All)	
Finance, investment, insurance and tax specialists	034 (All) 039 .40	039 .50
Personnel and industrial relations officers and managers	041 (All)	
Organisation and Methods, work study and operational research officers	042 (All)	
Economists, statisticians, actuaries	043 (All)	
Systems analysts and computer programmers	044 (All)	
Marketing and sales managers and executives	051 .05 051 .10	051 .15
Advertising and public relations managers and executives	051 .20 051 .25 051 .30	051 .35 051 .40 051 .45
Purchasing officers and buyers	061 (All)	
Property and estate managers	062 (All)	
Librarians and information officers	063 .10 063 .30	063 .40
Public health inspectors	064 .05	
Other statutory and similar inspectors	064 (All except 064 .05)	
Civil servants (administrative and executive functions) not identified elsewhere	069 .20	
Local government officers (administrative and executive functions) not identified elsewhere	069 .30	
All other professional and related supporting management and administration	023 (All) 029 (All) 039 (Pt)	049 (All) 063 (Pt) 069 (Pt)

GROUP III PROFESSIONAL AND RELATED IN EDUCATION, WELFARE AND HEALTH

University academic staff	091 (All)	
Teachers in establishments for further and higher education	092 (All)	093 (All)
Secondary teachers	094 (All)	
Primary teachers	095 (All)	
Pre-primary teachers	096 (All)	
Special education teachers	097 (All)	
Vocational/industrial trainers	098 (All)	
Directors of education, education officers, school inspectors	099 .00	099 .10
	099 .01	
Social and behavioural scientists	101 (All)	
Welfare workers (social, medical, industrial, educational and moral)	102 (All)	
Clergy, ministers of religion	103 (All)	
Medical practitioners	111 (All)	
Dental practitioners	112 (All)	
Nurse administrators and nurse executives	113 .02	113 .22
	113 .04	113 .24
	113 .06	113 .26
	113 .08	113 .28
	113 .10	113 .56
	113 .20	113 .70
State registered and state enrolled nurses and state certified midwives	113 .30	113 .54
	113 .32	113 .58
	113 .34	113 .60
	113 .50	113 .62
	113 .52	113 .64
Nursing auxiliaries and assistants	113 .36	
Pharmacists	114 (All)	
Medical radiographers	115 (All)	
Ophthalmic and dispensing opticians	116 (All)	
Remedial therapists	117 (All)	
Chiropodists	119 .10	
Medical technicians and dental auxiliaries	119 (All except	
	119 .05	119 .10)
Veterinarians	121 (All)	
All other professional and related in education, welfare and health	099 (Pt)	119 (Pt)
	109 (All)	129 (All)

GROUP IV LITERARY, ARTISTIC AND SPORTS

Authors, writers and journalists	151 (All)	159 (All)
Artists, commercial artists	161 (All)	
Industrial designers	162 (All)	
Actors, musicians, entertainers, stage managers	171 (All)	179 .10
	172 (All)	179 .20
	173 (All)	179 .30
Photographers and cameramen	174 (All)	
Sound and vision equipment operators	175 (All)	
Window dressers	179 .40	
Professional sportsmen, sports officials	181 (All)	
All other literary, artistic and sports	179 (Pt)	

Codot Unit Group/Occ No.

GROUP V PROFESSIONAL AND RELATED IN SCIENCE, ENGINEERING, TECHNOLOGY AND SIMILAR FIELDS

Notes

1. Includes (1) persons studying scientific phenomena (scientists) and persons applying scientific and other technical knowledge for commercial and industrial use and exploitation in engineering and other technologies (engineers and technologists). They manage, technically direct or undertake one or more of the following functions:

research, development, design, feasibility studies, applications, technical advisory and liaison, consultancy or similar work

(2) technicians supporting scientists, engineers and technologists

(3) certain "technical" occupations such as architects, surveyors, ships' and aircraft officers

2. Excludes persons holding professional qualifications in science, engineering and other technologies who are engaged in non-technical and non-scientific activities eg teaching, operational research, work study, statistics, technical representation, technical writing and management of non-technical and non-scientific activities (Groups I, II, III, VI and VIII)

Biological scientists and biochemists	211 (All)	219 .10
Chemical scientists	212 (All)	219 .30
Physical and geological scientists and mathematicians	213 (All)	215 (All)
	214 (All)	219 .20
Civil, structural and municipal engineers	221 (All)	
Mining, quarrying and drilling engineers	222 (All)	
Mechanical engineers	223 (All except	
	223 .14	223 .44
	223 .24	223 .54
	223 .34	223 .64
		223 .74)
Aeronautical engineers	223 .14	223 .54
	223 .24	223 .64
	223 .34	223 .74
	223 .44	
Electrical engineers		
Electronic engineers	224 (All)	
Electrical/Electronic Engineers		
Chemical engineers	225 (All)	
Production en gineers	226 (All)	
Planning and quality control engineers	259 .10	259 .40
Heating and ventilating engineers	229 .30	
General andother engineers	229 (All except	
	229 .30)	
Metallur gists	231 .05	
All other technologists	231 (All except	
	231 .05)	
Engineering draughtsmen	253 (All except	
	253 .32	253 .34
		253 .52)
Architectural and other draughtsmen	253 .32	253 .52
	253 .34	
Laboratory technicians (scientific and medical)	254 (All)	
Engineering technicians and technician engineers	256 (All)	
Architects and town planners	251 (All)	
Town planning assistants, architectural and building technicians	255 (All except	
	255 .10	255 .20)
Quantity surveyors	255 .10	255 .20
Building, land and mining surveyors	252 .10	252 .40
	252 .30	

Aircraft flight deck officers	241 (All)	
Air traffic planners and controllers	242 (All)	
Ships' masters, deck officers and pilots	243 (All)	
Ships' engineer officers	244 .10	244 .20
Ships' radio officers	244 .30	
All other professional and related in science, engineering and other technologies and similar fields	249 (All) 252 (Pt)	259 (Pt)

GROUP VI MANAGERIAL (EXCLUDING GENERAL MANAGEMENT)

Notes
1. *Includes works, general and other senior foremen, with foremen under their control*
2. *Excludes foremen (except works, general and other senior foremen), charge hands mainly engaged on supervision, and supervisors. These are separately identified as key occupations in various groups with the workers they control*

Production managers, works managers, works foremen	271 (All)	272 (All)
Engineering maintenance managers	273 (All)	
Site and other managers, agents and clerks of works, general foremen (building and civil engineering)	274 (All)	
Managers—underground mining and public utilities	275 (All)	276 (All)
Transport managers—air, sea, rail, road, harbour	277 (All except 277 .32 277 .36 277 .34 277 .38 277 .40)	
Managers—warehousing and materials handling	277 .32 277 .38 277 .34 277 .40 277 .36	
Office managers—national government Office managers—local government Other office managers	281 (All)	
Managers—wholesale distribution	282 (All)	
Managers—department store, variety chain store, supermarket and departmental managers	283 .10 283 .20	283 .50
Branch managers of shops other than above	283 .30	
Managers of independent shops (employees) Shop keepers (employers and self-employed)	283 .40	283 .60
Hotel and residential club managers	284 .05 284 .10	284 .15
Publicans (employers and self-employed) Publicans (employees)	284 .70	
Catering and non-residential club managers	284 .30 284 .55 284 .35 284 .60 284 .40 284 .65 284 .45 284 .80 284 .50	
Entertainment and sports managers	285 (All)	
Farmers and horticulturists (employers and self-employed) Farm managers (employees)	286 (All except 286 .40 286 .55 286 .50 286 .60)	
Officers (Armed Forces) not identified elsewhere (ie service officers with no civilian occupational counterpart)	287 (All)	
Police officers (inspectors and above)	288 .10	
Prison officers (chief officers and above)	288 .40	
Fire service officers	288 .20	288 .30
All other managers	279 (All) 288 (Pt) 284 (Pt) 289 (All) 286 (Pt)	

GROUP VII   CLERICAL AND RELATED

Supervisors of clerks	310 (All)	
Clerks	311 (All)	
	312 (All except	
	312.90	312.91)
	313 (All)	315 (All)
	314 (All)	316 (All)
	319 (All except	
	319.56	
	319.58	319.60)
Retail shop cashiers	312.90	
Retail shop check-out and cash and wrap operators	312.91	
Receptionists	319.56	319.60
	319.58	
Supervisors of typists, etc	320 (All)	
Personal secretaries, shorthand writers and shorthand typists	321 (All)	
Other typists	322 (All)	
Supervisors of office machine operators	330 (All)	
Office machine operators	331 (All)	334 (All)
	332 (All)	339 (All)
	333 (All)	
Supervisors of telephonists, radio and telegraph operators	340.10	340.30
	340.20	
Telephonists	341 (All)	
Radio and telegraph operators	342 (All)	
Supervisors of postmen, mail sorters and messengers	340.40	
Postmen, mail sorters and messengers	343 (All)	

GROUP VIII   SELLING

Sales supervisors	360 (All)	
Salesmen, sales assistants, shop assistants and shelf fillers	361 (All except	
	361.92)	369.99 (Pt)
Petrol pump/forecourt attendants	361.92	
Roundsmen and van salesmen	362 (All)	363.10
Technical sales representatives	371 (All)	
Sales representatives (wholesale goods)	372 (All)	
Other sales representatives and agents	363 (Pt)	373 (All)
	369 (Pt)	379 (All)

GROUP IX   SECURITY AND PROTECTIVE SERVICE

Non-commissioned Officers and Other Ranks (Armed Forces) not identified elsewhere ie with no civilian occupational counterpart	400 (All)	401 (All)
Supervisors (police sergeants, fire fighting and related)	410 (All)	
Policemen (below sergeant)	411 (All)	
Firemen	412 (All)	
Prison officers below principal officer	419.20	
Security officers and detectives	419.50	419.60
	419.55	419.65
Security guards, patrolmen	419.70	419.91
	419.75	419.92
	419.90	
Traffic wardens	419.93	
All other in security and protective service	419 (Pt)	

GROUP X CATERING, CLEANING, HAIRDRESSING AND OTHER PERSONAL SERVICE

Catering supervisors	430 (All)	
Chefs, cooks	431 (All)	
Waiters, waitresses	432 (All)	
Barmen, barmaids	433 (All)	
Counter hands/assistants	434 (All)	
Kitchen porters/hands	435 .10	435 .30
	435 .20	
Supervisors—housekeeping and related	440 (All)	
Domestic housekeepers	441 .05	
Home and domestic helpers, maids	441 .10	441 .55
	441 .15	441 .60
	441 .20	441 .75
	441 .25	441 .80
	441 .30	441 .85
School helpers and school supervisory assistants	441 .65	441 .70
Travel stewards and attendants	442 (All)	
Ambulancemen	443 .20	
Hospital/ward orderlies	443 .10	443 .40
	443 .30	443 .50
Hospital porters	449 .30	
Hotel porters	449 .10	449 .50
	449 .20	
Supervisors/foremen—caretaking, cleaning and related	450 (All)	
Caretakers	451 (All)	
Road sweepers (manual)	452 .60	
Other cleaners	452 (All except 452 .60)	
Railway stationmen	453 (All)	
Lift and car park attendants	459 .30	459 .45
Garment pressers	461 .08	461 .14
	461 .10	461 .16
	461 .12	
Hairdressing supervisors	470 .10	
Hairdressers (men), barbers	471 .10	
Hairdressers (ladies)	471 .05	
All other in catering, cleaning, hairdressing and other personal service	435 (Pt)	461 (Pt)
	439 (All)	470 (Pt)
	441 (Pt)	471 (Pt)
	459 (Pt)	472 (All)
	460 (All)	479 (All)

GROUP XI FARMING, FISHING AND RELATED

Foremen—farming, horticulture, forestry	500 (All)	
General farm workers	501 (All)	
Dairy cowmen	502 .04	
Pig and poultry men	502 .10	502 .50
Other stockmen	502 .02	502 .08
	502 .06	
Horticultural workers	503 (All)	
Domestic gardeners (private gardens)	504 .20	
Non-domestic gardeners and groundsmen	504 .10	504 .40
	504 .30	504 .50
Agricultural machinery drivers/operators	505 (All)	
Forestry workers	506 (All)	

Codot Unit Group/Occ No.

Supervisors/mates—fishing	510 (All)	
Fishermen	511 (All)	519 (All)
All other in farming and related	502 (Pt)	509 (All)

GROUP XII   MATERIALS PROCESSING (EXCLUDING METAL)

[hides, textiles, chemicals, food, drink and tobacco, wood, paper and board, rubber and plastics]

Foremen—tannery production workers	530 (All)	
Tannery production workers	531 (All)	
Foremen—textile processing	540 (All)	
Preparatory fibre processors	541 (All)	
Spinners, doublers/twisters	542.10	542.60
	542.50	542.70
	542.55	542.75
Winders, reelers	542.65	542.90
	542.80	542.92
Warp preparers	543 (All)	
Weavers	544 (All)	
Knitters	545 (All)	
Bleachers, dyers, finishers	546 (All except	
	546.50	546.86
	546.85	546.89)
Burlers, menders, darners	547 (All)	
Foremen—chemical processing	560 (All)	
Chemical, gas and petroleum process plant operators	561 (All)	
Foremen—food and drink processing	570 (All)	
Bread bakers (hand)	571.05	571.50
	571.15	
Flour confectioners	571.10	571.20
Butchers, meat cutters	572 (All)	
Foremen—paper and board making	580 (All)	
Beatermen, refinerman (paper and board making)	582.10	582.50
Machinemen, dryermen, calendermen, reelermen (paper and board making)	584.05	584.65
	584.10	584.80
Foremen—processing—glass, ceramics, rubber, plastics, etc	590 (All)	
Glass and ceramic furnacemen and kilnmen	591.10	591.58
	591.50	591.62
	591.52	591.90
	591.54	
Kiln setters	599.50	
Masticating millmen (rubber and plastics)	592.55	
Rubber mixers and compounders	592.70	
Calender and extruding machine operators (rubber and plastics)	594.60	594.62
Man-made fibre makers	594.58	
Sewage plant attendants	593.45	
All other in processing materials (other than metal)	546 (Pt)	581 (All)
	548 (All)	582 (Pt)
	549 (All)	583 (All)
	550 (All)	584 (Pt)
	551 (All)	589 (All)
	573 (All)	591 (Pt)
	574 (All)	592 (Pt)
	575 (All)	593 (Pt)
	576 (All)	594 (Pt)
	579 (All)	599 (Pt)

GROUP XIII MAKING AND REPAIRING (EXCLUDING METAL AND ELECTRICAL)

[glass, ceramics, printing, paper products, clothing, footwear, woodworking, rubber and plastics]

Foremen—glass working	610 (All)	
Glass formers and shapers	611 (All)	613 (All)
	612 (All)	
Glass finishers and decorators	614 (All)	
Foremen—clay and stone working	620 (All)	
Casters and other pottery makers	621 .06	621 .50
	*621 .08	621 .52
	*621 .10	621 .54
	*621 .16	*621 .58
	*621 .18	*621 .60
	621 .26	621 .90

*these CODOT definitions also cover ceramics other than pottery

Cutters, shapers and polishers (stone)	624 (All)	
Foremen—printing	630 (All)	
Compositors	631 (All)	632 (All)
Electrotypers, stereotypers	633 .02	633 .04
Other printing plate and cylinder preparers	633 .06	633 .12
	633 .08	633 .14
	633 .10	
Printing machine minders (letterpress)	634 .05	634 .10
,, ,, ,, (lithography)	634 .15	
,, ,, ,, (photogravure)	634 .20	
,, ,, assistants (letterpress, lithography, photogravure)	639 .50	639 .54
	639 .52	
Screen and block printers	635 (All)	
Foremen—bookbinding	640 .10	
Foremen—paper products making	640 .20	
Bookbinders and finishers	641 (All)	
Cutting and slitting machine operators (paper and paper products making)	642 .54	642 .56
Foremen—textile materials working	650 (All)	
Bespoke tailors and tailoresses	651 (All)	
Dressmakers	652 .10	652 .40
	652 .30	
Coach trimmers	653 .05	
Upholsterers, mattress makers	653 .10	653 .20
	653 .15	653 .60
Milliners	654 (All)	
Furriers	655 (All)	
Clothing cutters and markers (measure)	656 .10	656 .14
	656 .12	
Other clothing cutters and markers	656 .16	656 .52
	656 .18	656 .54
	656 .20	656 .56
	656 .50	656 .58
Hard sewers and embroiderers	657 (All)	
Linkers	658 .60	
Sewing machinists (textile materials)	658 (All except 658 .60)	

Note: For clothing pressers see Group X

Foremen—leather and leather substitutes working	660 (All)

KEY LIST

	Codot Unit Group/Occ No.	
Boot and shoe makers (bespoke) and repairers	661 (All)	666 (All)
Leather and leather substitutes—cutters	662 (All)	
Footwear lasters	663 (All)	
Leather and leather substitutes—sewers	665 (All)	
Footwear finishers	669 .14	669 .64
	669 .60	669 .66
	669 .62	669 .94
Foremen—woodworking	670 (All)	
Carpenters and joiners (construction sites and maintenance)	671 .05	671 .15
	671 .10	
Carpenters and joiners (ship and stage)	671 .20	671 .40
	671 .25	671 .45
	671 .35	
Carpenters and joiners (others)	671 .30	673 .20
	673 .05	673 .25
	673 .10	673 .30
	673 .15	
Cabinet makers	672 (All)	
Case and box makers	673 .40	673 .45
Wood sawyers and veneer cutters	674 (All)	
Woodworking machinists (setters and setter operators)	675 (All)	
Other woodworking machinists (operators and minders)	676 (All)	
Patternmakers (moulds)	677 (All)	
Labourers and mates to woodworking craftsmen	679 .90	679 .92
Foremen—rubber and plastics working	680 (All)	
Tyre builders	681 .06	
Moulding machine operators/attendants (rubber and plastics)	681 .60	681 .92
	681 .90	
Dental mechanics	692 .20	
All other in making and repairing (excluding metal and electrical)	619 (All)	656 (Pt)
	621 (Pt)	659 (All)
	622 (All)	664 (All)
	623 (All)	669 (Pt)
	629 (All)	673 (Pt)
	634 (Pt)	679 (Pt)
	636 (All)	681 (Pt)
	639 (Pt)	690 (All)
	642 (Pt)	691 (All)
	652 (Pt)	692 (Pt)
	653 (Pt)	699 (All)

GROUP XIV PROCESSING, MAKING, REPAIRING AND RELATED (METAL AND ELECTRICAL)

[iron, steel and other metals, engineering (including installation and maintenance) vehicles and shipbuilding]

Foremen—metal making and treating	710 (All)	
Blast furnacemen	711 .02	711 .52
	711 .04	
Furnacemen (steel smelting)	711 .08	711 .56
Other furnacemen (metal)	711 (All except	
	711 .02	711 .08
	711 .04	711 .52
		711 .56)
Rollermen (steel)	712 .05	712 .10
Metal drawers	712 .70	712 .75

Codot Unit Group/Occ No.

Moulders and moulder/coremakers	713 .05	713 .20
	713 .10	713 .25
	713 .15	
Machine moulders, shell moulders and machine coremakers	713 .50	713 .54
	713 .52	713 .92
Die casters	713 .68	713 .70
Smiths, forgemen	714 .05	714 .25
	714 .10	714 .30
	714 .15	714 .35
	714 .20	
Electroplaters	715 .05	
Annealers, hardeners, temperers (metal)	716 (All)	
Foremen—engineering machining	720 (All)	
Press and machine tool setters	721 (All)	
Roll turners, roll grinders	722 .08	722 .20
Other centre lathe turners	722 .04	
Machine tool setter operators	722 (All except	
	722 .04	
	722 .08	722 .20)
Machine tool operators (not setting-up)	723 (All)	
Press and stamping machine operators	724 (All)	
Automatic machine attendants/minders	725 (All)	
Metal polishers	726 .20	726 .55
	726 .50	726 .60
Fettlers/dressers	726 .90	
Foremen—production fitting (metal)	730 (All)	
Toolmakers, tool fitters, markers-out	731 (All)	
Precision instrument makers	732 (All)	
Metal working production fitters (fine limits)	733 (All except	
	733 .50)	
Metal working production fitter-machinists (fine limits)	733 .50	
Other metal working production fitters (not to fine limits)	734 (All)	
Foremen—installation and maintenance—machines and instruments	740 (All)	
Machinery erectors and installers	741 .02	741 .06
	741 .04	
Maintenance fitters (non-electrical) plant and industrial machinery	741 (All except	
	741 .02	741 06
	741 .04	741 .26)
Knitting machine mechanics (industrial)	741 .26	
Motor vehicle mechanics (skilled)	742 (All)	
Other motor vehicle mechanics	746 .10	
Maintenance and service fitters (aircraft engines)	743 (All)	
	749 .05	
Watch and clock repairers	744 .30	
Instrument mechanics	744 (All except	
	744 .30)	
Office machinery mechanics	745 (All)	
Foremen—production fitting and wiring (electrical/electronic)	750 (All)	
Production fitters (electrical/electronic)	751 (All)	
Production electricians	752 (All)	
Foremen—installation and maintenance—electrical/electronic	760 (All)	
Electricians (installation and maintenance) plant and machinery	761 (All)	
Electricians (installation and maintenance) premises and ships	762 (All)	
Telephone fitters	763 .10	

KEY LIST

Radio, TV and other electronic maintenance fitters and mechanics	763 (All except 763 .10)	
Cable jointers and linesmen	764 (All)	
Foremen/supervisors—metal working—pipes, sheets, structures	770 (All)	
Plumbers, pipe fitters	771 .05	771 .30
	771 .10	771 .35
	771 .15	
Heating and ventilating engineering fitters	771 .25	
Gas fitters	771 .20	
Sheet metal workers	772 (All)	
Platers and metal shipwrights	773 .02	773 .08
	773 .04	773 .10
	773 .06	773 .12
Caulker burners, riveters and drillers (constructional metal)	773 .14	773 .18
	773 .16	
General steelworkers (shipbuilding and repair)	773 .20	
Steel erectors	774 .20	
Scaffolders/stagers	774 .25	774 .30
Steel benders, bar benders and fixers	774 .50	
Welders (skilled)	775 .05	775 .25
	775 .10	775 .30
	775 .15	775 .35
	775 .20	
Other welders	775 .50	775 .92
	775 .90	
Foremen—other processing, making and repairing (metal and electrical)	790 (All)	
Goldsmiths, silversmiths and precious stone workers	791 (All)	
Engravers and etchers (printing)	792 .02	792 .10
	792 .04	792 .12
	792 .06	792 .14
	792 .08	792 .16
Coach and vehicle body builders/makers	793 .10	793 .20
Aircraft finishers	793 .30	
Maintenance and installation fitters (mechanical *and* electrical)	799 .02	799 .04
Setter operators of woodworking *and* metal working machines	799 .06	
All other skilled in processing, making and repairing (metal and electrical) ⎫	712 (Pt)	759 (All)
All other non-skilled in processing, making and repairing (metal and electrical) ⎭	713 (Pt)	769 (All)
	714 (Pt)	771 (Pt)
	715 (Pt)	773 (Pt)
	719 (All)	774 (Pt)
	726 (Pt)	776 (All)
	729 (All)	779 (All)
	739 (All)	792 (Pt)
	746 (Pt)	799 (Pt)
	749 (Pt)	

GROUP XV PAINTING, REPETITIVE ASSEMBLING, PRODUCT INSPECTING, PACKAGING AND RELATED

Foremen—painting and similar coating	810 (All)	
Painters and decorators	811 (All)	812 .05
Pottery decorators	*812 .15	*813 .50
	*812 .20	*813 .90
	*812 .25	*814 .10
	*812 .50	*819 .10

continued

Codot Unit Group/Occ No.

Pottery decorators *continuea*	*812 .60 *819 .55
	*812 .90 *819 .92
	*these CODOT definitions also cover ceramics other than pottery

As appropriate

Coach painters	813 .10 813 .70
Other spray painters	813 .20 813 .75
	813 .55 813 .92
	813 .60 819 .20
	813 .65
French polishers	815 .10
Foremen—product assembling (repetitive)	820 (All)
Repetitive assemblers (metal and electrical goods)	821 .35 821 .45
	821 .40
Foremen—product inspection	830 (All)
Inspectors and testers (skilled) (metal and electrical engineering)	831 (All)
Viewers (metal and electrical engineering)	832 (All)
Foremen—packaging	840 (All)
Packers, bottlers, canners, fillers	841 (All) 842 (All)
All other in painting, repetitive assembling, product inspecting, packaging and related	812 (Pt) 833 (All)
	814 (Pt) 834 (All)
	819 (Pt) 835 (All)
	821 (Pt) 839 (All)

GROUP XVI CONSTRUCTION, MINING AND RELATED NOT IDENTIFIED ELSEWHERE

Note: Excludes joiners and other woodworkers (Group XIII), electricians, plumbers, heating and ventilating fitters, steel erectors and scaffolders (Group XIV), painters and decorators (Group XV), civil engineering plant drivers/operators (Group XVIII) and labourers/mates to these craftsmen (see Groups concerned)

Foremen—building and civil engineering not identified elsewhere	860 (All)
Bricklayers	861 .10 861 .30
	861 .20 861 .50
Fixer/walling masons	861 .40
Plasterers	862 (All)
Floor and wall tilers, terrazzo workers	863 (All)
Roofers and slaters	864 (All)
Glaziers	865 (All)
Railway lengthmen	866 .20 866 .30
Asphalt and bitumen road surfacers	866 .60 866 .90
Other roadmen	866 .10 866 .92
	866 .50
Concrete erectors/assemblers	867 (All)
Concrete levellers/screeders	869 .54
General builders	869 .02
Sewermen (maintenance)	869 .20
Mains and service layers and pipe jointers (gas, water, drainage, oil)	869 .28 869 .32
	869 .30
Waste inspectors (water supply)	869 .34
Craftsmen's mates and other builders' labourers not identified elsewhere	868 (All except
	868 .60 868 .70)

	Codot Unit Group/Occ No.	
Civil engineering labourers	868 .60	868 .70
Foremen/deputies—coalmining	870 .30	
Face-trained coalmining workers	871 .05	873 (All)
	871 .15	879 .20
	872 .10	879 .30
Tunnellers	872 .20	
All other in construction, mining, quarrying, well drilling and related, not identified elsewhere	869 (Pt)	871 (Pt)
	870 (Pt)	879 (Pt)

GROUP XVII TRANSPORT OPERATING, MATERIALS MOVING AND STORING AND RELATED

Note: Excludes ships' and aircraft officers (Group V) and railway stationmen and railway station foremen (Group X)

Foremen—ships, lighters and other vessels	910 (All)	
Deck and engine-room hands (sea-going)	911 (All except 911 .15)	
Bargemen, lightermen, boatmen, tugmen	911 .15	
Foremen—rail transport operating	920 (All)	
Railway engine drivers, motormen	921 (All except 921 .20)	
Secondmen (railways)	921 .20	
Railway guards	922 (All)	
Railway signalmen and shunters	923 (All)	
Foremen—road transport operating	930 (All except 930 .10)	
Bus inspectors	930 .10	
Bus and coach drivers	931 (All)	
Heavy goods drivers (over 3 tons unladen weight)	932 (All)	
Other goods drivers	933 .10	
Other motor drivers	933 (All except 933 .10)	
Bus conductors	934 (All)	
Drivers' mates	935 (All)	
Foremen—civil engineering plant operating	940 .10	
Mechanical plant drivers/operators (earth moving and civil engineering)	941 (All)	
Foremen—materials handling equipment operating	940 .20	
Crane drivers/operators	942 .05	942 .54
	942 .10	942 .56
	942 .30	942 .58
	942 .50	942 .60
	942 .52	
Fork lift and other mechanical truck drivers/operators	942 .62	942 .66
	942 .64	942 .74
Foremen—materials moving and storing	950 (All)	
Storekeepers, warehousemen	951 (All)	
Stevedores and dockers	952 (All)	
Furniture removers	959 .10	
Warehouse, market and other goods porters	959 .50	959 .70
	959 .65	
Refuse collectors/dustmen	959 .85	
All other in transport operating, materials moving and storing and related not identified elsewhere	919 (All)	942 (Pt)
	939 (All)	949 (All)
		959 (Pt)

GROUP XVIII MISCELLANEOUS

Note: This group caters for occupations not identified in Groups I to XVII

Foremen—miscellaneous	970 (All)	990 (All)
Electricity power plant operators and switchboard attendants	971 .05	971 .55
	971 .10	973 .10
	*971 .15	973 .50
	*971 .20	979 .10

*these CODOT definitions also cover power generating other than by electricity

Turncocks (water supply)	972 .60	
General labourers (engineering and shipbuilding)	991 .10	991 .20
Other general labourers		
All other in miscellaneous occupations not identified elsewhere	971 (Pt)	979 (Pt)
	972 (Pt)	991 (Pt)

INDEX OF TITLES

Notes: (1) *for general guidance see introduction, pages 19-20*

(2) *all occupational groups with the title "other . . . ." are sub-classified* .99 *in the appropriate main classification and have therefore not been included but occupations in these groups which have been allocated specific titles are included*

(3) *nec=not elsewhere classified.*

Att (*continued*)

†Unit Group

†Unit Group

Calender hand
  laundering.................... 461.70
  linoleum..................... 594.92
  textile finishing 546.91
Calender machine assistant
  paper........................ 589.99
  paperboard 589.99
Calenderer
  asbestos composition.......... 594.90
  coated fabric making.......... 549.12
  textile finishing 546.91
Calenderhand
  plastics 594.60
  rubber...................... 594.60
Calenderman
  asbestos composition.......... 594.90
  plastics 594.60
  rubber...................... 594.60
Calibrator 732.99
Call boy...................... 449.99
Caller, bingo.................. 479.55
Camera assistant, films 174.50
Cameraman
  chief, films 171.25
  film 174.40
  film, assistant 174.50
  first 171.25
  lighting 171.25
  television................... 174.30
Can dodger.................... 541.55
Canal maintenance worker 869.99
Candler, egg.................. 833.99
Canner
  beverages 842.40
  chemical products 842.50
  foodstuffs 842.40
  lubricants 842.50
Canroyer...................... 546.90
Canteen assistant.............. 434.30
Canvasser
  door-to-door
    goods..................... 379.90
    household services........... 379.95
Capper
  bottling 842.30
  electric lamp................ 821.45
  paper....................... 841.99
Captain
  canal craft.................. 243.30
  dock craft 243.30
  foreign-going ship 243.10
  harbour craft 243.30
  home trade ship.............. 243.20
  hovercraft 249.10
  inland waterways craft 243.30
  river craft 243.30
  Salvation Army 103.10
  staff, passenger vessel 243.10
Car lasher.................... 952.99
Carbon printer, photogravure 633.10
Carbonatation man, sugar 576.74
Carbonation and filtration man
  ciders...................... 576.76
  wines...................... 576.76
Carboniser
  metal....................... 716.50
  textiles..................... 546.85

Card dresser.................. 799.50
Card fillet dresser 799.50
Card puller................... 316.90
Card top clipper 799.52
Carder
  addressing machine 339.10
  attending fibre carding machine 541.10
  pelts....................... 531.93
  under, in charge of fibre preparers ... 540.05
Cardiologist 111.10
Care assistant 443.50
Careers officer 109.10
Caretaker
  church...................... 451.10
  premises excluding churches 451.20
  reservoir 869.64
†Caretakers................... 451
*Caretaking, cleaning and attending
  occupations, premises and property 45
Carman
  charger
    coal-gas oven 942.66
    coke oven 942.66
  coke
    coal-gas oven 942.74
    coke oven 942.74
  transfer 942.66
Carpenter
  colliery 671.05
  construction 671.10
  formwork 671.15
  jobbing 671.05
  ship's...................... 671.20
  stage 671.25
  studio 671.25
Carpenter and joiner.......... 671.05
†Carpenters, and carpenters and joiners,
  structural woodworking 671
Carpenter's mate 679.90
Carrier
  bobbin...................... 959.55
  glass....................... 959.55
  lap 959.55
  ware, pottery manufacture 959.55
Carrier-in
  kiln 599.99
  lehr 599.99
Carrotter..................... 531.93
Carter 939.10
Cartoner
  hand, chemical pharmaceutical and
    allied products 841.15
  machine..................... 842.10
Cartoonist.................... 161.20
Carver
  food........................ 439.10
  stone 624.08
  wood 679.05
Case hand..................... 632.10
Caser, die 799.99
Caseworker
  family 102.04
  social, general.............. 102.02
Cash and wrap assistant 312.91
†Cash handling clerical occupations 312

†Unit Group

Cle (*continued*)

*Minor Group   †Unit Group

Conductor: *continued*

  orchestra 173.10

  public service vehicle 934.10

  vocal group 173.99

Conductor guard 922.10

†Conductors, road transport 934

Coner

  bristle 549.99

  hat making 659.10

Confectioner, flour 571.10

Conformer

  insole 669.52

  sole 669.52

Conjurer 173.80

Constable

  police

    airport 411.20

    civil police 411.10

    docks 411.20

    excluding civil police........... 411.20

    railway...................... 411.20

Constructional plater's helper 776.30

Constructor, map.................. 253.34

Consultant

  actuarial 043.30

  beauty......................... 361.20

  business efficiency 042.10

  dental 112.10

  diseases of the chest 111.10

  economic....................... 043.10

  engineering—see Engineer,
    consultancy and advice

  gynaecology and obstetrics.......... 111.20

  infectious diseases 111.10

  organisation and methods.......... 042.10

  physical medicine and rehabilitation.. 111.10

  statistical 043.20

  tax 039.50

  work study 042.15

Consultant anaesthetist.............. 111.25

Consultant physician................ 111.10

Consultant psychiatrist 111.30

Consultant radiologist............... 111.35

Consultant surgeon 111.15

Contact man, advertising 051.25

Continuous cleaning plant assistant,
  metal 719.82

Continuous cut-up line assistant, metal . 729.90

Contractor, electrical............... 224.12

Control assistant

  air traffic...................... 342.40

  passenger 442.99

  sensitometric 636.06

Control man

  bunker

    gravel....................... 942.78

    sand........................ 942.78

    surface, mining 942.20

    underground, mining 942.15

Controller

  advance, banking 034.99

  air, aerodrome 242.40

  approach procedure, air traffic....... 242.40

  approach radar, aerodrome.......... 242.40

  apron.......................... 959.99

  area procedure, air traffic 242.30

Controller: *continued*

  area radar, air traffic 242.30

  coal washing and mixing plant 594.99

  credit.......................... 281.06

  depot, distribution................. 277.32

  financial........................ 032.20

  flight information, region 242.30

  ground movement, aerodrome....... 242.40

  inventory....................... 277.34

  load, air transport 315.15

  management services.............. 049.10

  materials 277.34

  movements, air flights............. 242.20

  oceanic air traffic 242.30

  plasterboard making machine 594.56

  precision landing, aerodrome........ 242.40

  process, hides skins pelts 272.51

  production—see Manager, production
    control

  site............................ 274.10

  stock 277.34

  stores.......................... 277.36

  technical, installation—see 256

  transport, company transport....... 277.08

  zone, aerodrome................. 242.40

Controller of distribution 277.32

Controlman, steel converter.......... 711.56

Converter

  first hand, steel furnace 711.08

  second hand, steel furnace 711.56

  third hand, steel furnace 711.56

Converter man, chemicals 561.50

Conveyor mover.................... 749.70

Cook

  assistant........................ 431.90

  breakfast 431.10

  cheese, processed cheese manufacture. 573.58

  commis 431.98

  foreign fare..................... 431.15

  griddle......................... 431.99

  grill 431.10

  head

    club 430.10

    hotel 430.10

    industrial catering 430.20

    institutional catering 430.20

    restaurant 430.10

  luncheon....................... 431.10

  pastry, plain fare 431.30

  plain fare....................... 431.10

  private household 431.20

  ship's galley 431.25

  staff........................... 431.10

  vegetable....................... 431.90

Cooker

  fish............................ 573.54

  fruit........................... 573.54

  meat........................... 573.54

  potato crisp

    automatic equipment............. 576.85

    non-automatic equipment......... 573.99

  unspecified 591.68

  vegetables 573.54

  yeast food 573.99

Cook-general 431.20

Cook-housekeeper 441.05

†Unit Group

Cut (*continued*)

E

†Unit Group

*Minor Group   †Unit Group

Fitter-machinist: *continued*

door frame	734.30
engineering	733.50
gun, bespoke	733.50
lock	734.30
metal working	734.30
safe	734.30
staircase	734.30
weighing machines	733.50

Fitter-mechanic

agricultural machinery	741.18
coin-operated machines excluding weighing machines	741.34
locks	741.30
weighing machines	741.32
†Fitter-mechanics, motor vehicles	742
Fitter-mechanic's mate	799.90

Fitter's mate

gas	776.20
heating and ventilating engineering	776.10
maintenance	799.90
mechanical engineering	799.90
pipe	776.10
Fitter-turner	733.50

Fitter-up

bespoke tailoring	656.54
case maker's	821.25
piano	672.30
wholesale clothing	821.99
Fitter-welder, heating and ventilating	771.25

Fixer

bespoke tailoring	656.54
billiard table	699.04
blind	869.16
brush handle, wood	821.25
canvas	656.54
ceiling	869.14
lead light	865.10
lens, ophthalmic prescription	699.08
metal window	869.99
meter	769.20
mosaic	863.40
net	549.58
photographic processing	636.99
plasterboard	869.58
rate	042.25
roofing felt	864.30
sheet, roofs exterior walls	864.40
tape, paper patterns	642.58
tile	863.30

Fixer's mate

roofing felt	868.16
sheet	868.18
Flag officer, HMF	001.99

Flagger

bristle	541.30
fibre	541.30
hair	541.30
paving stones	866.10
Flaker-on, lead press	712.60
Flanger, hat	659.50

Flattener

pin	724.50
wire	729.65
Flatter, painting	819.94
Flautist	173.20

Flavouring man, cereal manufacture	574.99
Flayer	572.10
Fleecer, cotton wool	549.99
Flesher, hand	531.99
†Flight deck officers	241
Flight operations officer	242.20
Flight sergeant nec	400.10
Flipper, bead, rubber tyre	681.99
Flock fieldsman	502.99
Floor moulder	713.10

Floorman

asphalt	599.99
drilling rig	871.10
race course	312.92
Florist	179.50
Florist's assistant, retail trade	361.30
Fluffer	531.70

Fly hand

photogravure	639.54
rotary press	639.50
Flyman	991.30
Foiler, plasterboard	594.99

Folder

blouse	841.50
circular	319.90
dress	841.50
footwear	669.54
hand, fabric lapping	549.99
laundry, hand	841.50
machine, calender, laundering	461.70
paper pattern	821.99
paperboard containers	821.10
rag book	641.99
shirt	841.50
textile packaging, hand	841.50
yarn	542.65
Folder-in, gloves	821.99
†Food and beverage dispensers and counter hands, catering services	434
*Food and beverage preparing serving and related occupations	43
*Food and drink processing occupations	57
Food preparation assistant, cafeteria	431.90
Footballer, professional, Association	181.20
Footblower	611.50
Footmaker	611.50
Footman	441.99

Forcer

plastics	594.62
rubber	594.62
Fore hand, rope making	548.50
Forecaster, weather	213.65
Fore-end worker, rope making	548.50
Foregear man	548.50
Foreign exchange manager	034.99

Foreman

directly supervising—see first unit group, third digit 'O', in minor group for workers supervised general, construction	274.25
Forest officer	286.50
Forest worker, excluding nursery worker	506.10
Forester, Forestry Commission	500.80
Forge hammerman	714.10
Forge pressman	714.15

Grinder: *continued*

chocolate 574.52
cocoa 574.52
coffee 574.52
crankshaft, setter-operator 722.18
crook 622.10
cutlery
  hand 726.05
  machine 723.58
cylindrical, setter-operator 722.18
edge, abrasive wheel 623.28
edge tool
  hand 726.05
  machine 723.58
external, setter-operator 722.18
file, machine 723.58
flock 541.70
hand
  glass 614.65
  metal 726.05
internal, setter-operator 722.18
machine
  glass 614.70
    terrazzo tiles or slabs 624.65
malt 574.50
mill, unspecified 592.60
needle 726.99
optical glass lump 613.55
plain, setter-operator 722.18
porcelain 622.10
pottery 622.10
precision, setter-operator 722.18
provender milling 574.52
rag 541.70
refire 622.10
roll 722.20
roller covering 669.50
rotary, setter-operator 722.18
saw, machine 723.58
scissors, hand 726.05
shoddy 541.70
steel dressing 726.65
surface, setter-operator 722.18
tool and cutter, setter-operator 722.18
tool room, setter-operator 722.18
universal, setter-operator 722.18
unspecified, materials processing 592.60
Grinder and polisher
optical element, hand 613.15
optical slab 613.10
Grinderman, grain milling 574.52
Gripper, golf club 699.93
Gristman, brewing 574.50
Grog mill worker 599.99
Grommeter, light clothing 821.15
Groom 502.16
Groover, pencil 676.20
Grounder
fur 819.99
wallpaper 819.25
Groundlayer 819.10
Groundlayer's assistant 819.99
Groundskeeper 504.50
Groundsman 504.50
Grower
bulb 503.99
mushroom 503.99

Grower: *continued*

osier 506.99
watercress 503.99
Guard
building site 419.65
life, beach patrol 419.99
loco, mine 922.40
personal 419.75
premises 419.65
security 419.75
surface railway 922.20
train, ropes 949.65
underground railway excluding mine . 922.30
valuables in transit 419.75
Guarder 549.58
†Guards, rail transport 922
Guide
store 479.50
tour 442.40
Guide man, coke 949.60
Guillotineman
paper 642.54
paperboard 642.54
Guitarist 173.20
Gummer, coal mining 873.30
Gunner 401.10
Gutman 572.99
Gutter
fish
  hand 572.60
  machine 572.90
Gymnast, remedial 117.20
Gynaecologist 111.20

H

Hackler
hand 541.99
machine 541.10
Hackling machine attendant's assistant . 549.99
Hafter, razor 799.99
Hairdresser
ladies' 471.05
men's 471.10
†Hairdressing and beauty treatment
  occupations 471
*Hairdressing and miscellaneous service
  occupations 47
Hammerer, saw 799.14
Hammerman
forge 714.10
gold silver 791.02
pile-driving 941.10
white metal 791.02
Hander, tobacco 551.99
Handler
edge tool 821.25
materials, works 959.55
pottery 821.05
saw 821.25
shovel 821.25
tanyard 531.60
Handyman, residential establishment . . . 869.68
Hanger-up, hides skins pelts 531.92

*Minor Group   †Unit Group

I

†Unit Group

†Unit Group

Mak (*continued*)

Man (*continued*)

Man (*continued*)

        *Minor Group   †Unit Group

Ope (*continued*)

Ope (continued)

Ope (*continued*)

Ope (*continued*)

*Minor Group   †Unit Group

          †Unit Group

Seeker, gut	594.99
Seismologist	213.75
Selector	
ceramics	834.70
merchandise	061.10
optical glass	613.50
textile bags	834.55
textile sacks	834.55
Self-service laundry assistant	461.18
Seller	
programme	369.99
space	373.50
totalisator	312.60
*Selling occupations, distributive trade	36
Semantician	101.50
Senior officer	
fire brigade	288.20
police force	288.10
salvage corps	288.30
Senior ordinary seaman	911.10
Senior railman	453.10
Sensitometric control assistant	636.06
Separator	
ore, magnetic	593.15
plate, car battery	821.45
stitch, footwear	669.64
Sergeant	
police	
civil	410.10
excluding civil police	410.20
†Sergeants and other supervisors, police,	
firefighting and related protective	
service occupations	410
Serrater, cutlery	726.05
Service hand	
hotel	434.10
restaurant	434.10
Service man	
gas appliances	741.50
motor vehicles	746.10
oil burner	741.60
Serviceman	
accumulator	699.02
domestic television receivers	763.70
organ	691.20
railway carriage	452.30
Servicer, screen printing	639.99
†Servicing, oiling, greasing and related	
occupations, mechanical	746
Servitor, hand glass making	611.05
Setter	
assistant temper, iron and steel	821.35
barrel	799.10
beam	549.99
block	861.99
brick, fire-brick	861.20
capstan	721.10
chenille	544.99
circle comb	749.30
comber	741.24
diamond	
excluding industrial	791.32
industrial	791.34
die, press	721.30
edge	
hand, footwear	669.99
machine, footwear	669.62

Setter: *continued*	
faller	749.30
frame	
cycle	799.58
lace	546.99
metal bedsteads	799.99
gem	791.32
hat brim	659.50
jewel, watches	821.40
kiln	599.50
lens	619.10
machine	
automatic latch needle making	721.99
broaching	721.10
continuous casting	719.99
drawing	543.15
file cutting	721.99
paper products	642.05
paperboard products	642.05
unspecified, making or repairing,	
excluding metal and electrical	699.76
woodcutting	675.05
machine tool	
electrochemical	721.20
excluding electrochemical machine	
tools	721.10
needle, textile machinery	749.30
pattern, lace	741.24
pin, textile machinery	749.30
press	
extrusion, electrode coating	699.60
hand, fly	721.30
power	721.30
press tool	721.30
saw	729.99
spool, Axminster carpet	543.65
yarn	546.52
Setter drawer, kiln	599.50
Setter fitter mechanic,	
industrial knitting machines	741.26
textile machinery, excluding knitting	
machines	741.24
unspecified industrial machinery	741.28
Setter-in, razor	799.99
Setter-operator	
bakery equipment	576.50
lathe	
capstan	722.06
centre	722.04
roll turning	722.08
turret	722.06
wood turning	675.25
machine	
boring	
metal	722.12
wood	675.15
broaching	722.26
chainmaking, small links	729.02
cutting	
cork	699.58
gear	722.28
debarking	675.50
die-sinking	722.30
dovetailing	675.15
drilling, metal	722.10
engraving, pantograph, excluding	
printing plates and rollers	792.20

†Unit Group

†Unit Group

†Unit Group

W

*Minor Group

Terms used in some CODOT definitions in a particular or unusual sense

Articulator, a hinged metal device on which plaster moulds of teeth and gums are mounted to simulate patient's mouth.

Binder, tobacco leaf used to hold inner parts of cigar in place before wrapping.

Blocked optical lens, optical lens blank mounted in a carrier to facilitate grinding and polishing operations.

Broaching, a method of removing metal from a workpiece by the action of a tapered tool or "broach" provided with cutting teeth and resembling a coarse rasp.

Bushings, a metal device with numerous small holes in the base through which molten glass is extruded in the manufacture of glass fibres.

Calibration, a method of correcting or adjusting the graduations on the scale of a measuring instrument.

Card clothing, a series of wire teeth set into a foundation consisting of several layers of fabric and rubber or other vulcanising material.

Char, in sugar and glucose manufacture, bone-char or charcoal through which sugar or glucose liquor is filtered for purification and decolorization.

Chill, a piece of metal set into a mould to speed up the cooling of the casting and ensure even cooling by conducting heat from the thicker parts of the casting.

Circle, part of a fibre preparing machine consisting of a flat brass ring set with concentric rows of pins.

Cladding, the non-load bearing covering of walls and roofs of buildings.

Compressor, a pump for raising the pressure of a gas.

Continuous filament, a man-made fibre of indefinite length.

Counterbore, to enlarge the diameter of the end of a hole by boring.

Creel, a stand which holds supply packages for textile processing.

Cupellation, the metallurgical operation involved in the recovery of gold and silver from lead.

Dent, in weaving, the space between two wires of a reed (qv) through which warp threads are drawn.

Departmental store, a large shop with easily recognisable, distinctly separate departments, selling a wide range of goods, one of which must be clothing.

Die. 1. A metal block, fitted to a press or power hammer, with a particular shape cut into it. At each stroke of the press or hammer the die reproduces this shape on a blank of metal or other material.

2. A tool with internal cutting edges used to cut external screw threads.

Dividing head, a special attachment for machine tools which enables grooves to be cut and faces machined with a specified angle between them.

Dropper, a metal pin which causes a loom to stop if warp thread breaks.

Fairface, a brickwork surface which is built neatly and smoothly.

Faller, part of a fibre preparing machine consisting of a steel bar set with rows of pins.

Fettling, the removal of excess metal and sand from a casting.

Filler, the tobacco used for the inner parts of cigars.

Flat, a tool of quartz or glass whose surface is polished to very close tolerances. It is used as a precise measuring gauge of the flatness of surfaces by the reflection of light.

Float glass, flat glass manufactured by floating hot glass on a bath of heated liquid of greater density.

Focimeter, an instrument used to establish the optical centre of a lens.

Foreign going vessel, a ship travelling between a United Kingdom port and a port outside the United Kingdom, Channel Islands, Isle of Man, Irish Republic or Europe between Brest and the river Elbe.

Forme. 1. In printing, type and other matter locked in a metal frame ready for printing.

2. A wooden frame holding knives and metal rules for cutting and creasing paperboard.

Heald, on a weaving machine, a cord or wire with an eyelet in the centre through which a warp thread is passed before being drawn through the reed (qv).

Heald shaft, a frame on which healds are mounted.

Home trade vessel, a ship travelling between United Kingdom ports or between a United Kingdom port and a port in the Channel Islands, Isle of Man, Irish Republic or Europe between Brest and the river Elbe.

Honing, a method of machining to achieve a high quality mirror finish using a number of fine

continued

abrasive stones. It is particularly applicable to internal work eg cylinder bores.

Impression cylinder, a cylinder on a printing press which presses the material to be printed against the printing surface.

Jig board, a board used as a base for building up electrical wiring harness.

Lamina, tobacco leaf from which the stem has been removed.

Languid, a flat piece of metal or "tongue" which is soldered across the inside of an organ pipe about level with the aperture.

Lapping, a hand or machine technique employed as a finishing process using a block or disc of soft metal or wood (the lap) and a fine abrasive powder.

Launder, in metal processing, the channel down which molten metal flows from a furnace after tapping.

Lease cords/rods, in weaving, cords or rods used to separate warp threads and keep them in their proper order.

Letterpress, a relief printing process, ie the printing surface stands above the surrounding non-printing area.

Lithography, a planographic printing process, ie printing from a flat surface. The printing area is treated so that it accepts ink (which is greasy) while the non-printing area is damped and resists the ink. Lithographic printing is usually offset, ie the print is transferred from the printing plate on to a blanket cylinder which in turn offsets the ink impression on to the material to be printed.

Mimic diagram, an animated diagram of coloured lights, recorders or instruments, which indicates to the attendant the state of operations in a large process plant or transport network.

Package. 1. A holder on which fibrous strands or yarn are wound.

2. Fibrous strands or yarn wound on to a holder.

Photogravure, a printing process in which the printing area is sunk below the surface of the plate or cylinder.

Pick, in weaving, a single thread of weft.

Plasma, very hot ionised gas.

Process engraving, photo-engraving, the process in which relief printing plates are produced photographically and by etching.

Radial arm drill, a large drilling machine on which an arm swivels on a vertical supporting column. The drill spindle is fixed to a carriage on this arm and can be located at any point along it.

Radio-isotope, an element rendered radio-active and used in tracer-techniques (qv).

Reed, in weaving. 1. A device consisting of a number of wires fixed in a frame used to separate warp threads, to regulate the spacing of warp threads and to close up the weft.

2. To draw warp ends through reed.

Riser, in metal manufacture, a channel cut in a mould from the mould cavity to the surface. It acts as a reservoir for molten metal which feeds the casting as it cools and contracts.

Roving, in fibre preparing, fine fibrous strands produced in the later and/or final stages preparatory to spinning.

Scarfing, the removal by burning of defective area from semi-finished steel during manufacture.

Screed, a layer of mortar laid to finish a floor surface.

Sintering. 1. The fusing together of small particles of ore to form a larger mass.

2. The fusing together of metallic powders under heat and pressure.

Sliver, in fibre processing, a strand of fibres in rope form without twist.

Slubbing, in fibre processing. 1. A thick fibrous strand produced in the early stages of drawing preparatory to spinning.

2. Strips of fibrous web consolidated into strands by rubbing ready for spinning.

Staple fibre, man-made fibre cut or broken into suitable length for preparation and conversion into yarn by traditional textile processing methods.

Stellite, a type of very hard alloy.

Supermarket, a large self-service shop selling a full range of foods and some non-foods and of a specified minimum area.

Synchroscope, an instrument indicating the difference in frequency between two supplies of alternating current.

Tensioner, a device on a wheel spoke which can be tightened or loosened to adjust the tension on the spoke.

Tracer techniques, the monitoring of radio-active materials, for example in their passage through the body.

Variety chain store, one of a multiple organisation of stores, usually with a high degree of standardisation, selling a variety of goods.

Warp knitting, a form of knitting in which the loops made from each warp thread are formed along the length of the fabric.

Weft knitting, a form of knitting in which the loops made by each weft thread are formed across the width of the fabric.

Printed in England for Her Majesty's Stationery Office by McCorquodale Printers Ltd., London
HM 0110   Dd 0595532   K12   1/79   McC3309